THE ARCHITECTURE
OF THE OLD SOUTH

LONDON : GEOFFREY CUMBERLEGE
OXFORD UNIVERSITY PRESS

THE ARCHITECTURE
OF THE OLD SOUTH

The Medieval Style
1585–1850

BY

HENRY CHANDLEE FORMAN

HARVARD UNIVERSITY PRESS
CAMBRIDGE, MASSACHUSETTS
1948

To

LEICESTER BODINE HOLLAND
IN FRIENDSHIP

Contents

Foreword by Charles Rufus Morey xi

Acknowledgments xiii

PART I

OUR ENGLISH GOTHIC HERITAGE

CHAPTER

   I. The Field of the Cloth of Gold 3

  II. Before the Curtain Rose at Jamestown 6

PART II

VIRGINIA MEDIEVAL ARCHITECTURE

     I. The Beginning of American Architecture 9

    II. A Landscape of Wooden Chimneys 20

  III. The Virginia House Transplanted from England 25

  IV. The Virginia Town House 28

   V. How the Medieval Country House Developed 36

  VI. The Typical Country House in Virginia 47

 VII. The Cross-House in Virginia 54

VIII. The Crossroads Church 80

  IX. The Persistence of the Medieval Style into the Nineteenth Century . 86

   X. A Summary of the Virginia Style 98

PART III

MARYLAND MEDIEVAL ARCHITECTURE

I. Castle and Cot in Old St. Mary's City 107

II. The Maryland House Transplanted from England 113

III. The Town House of the Early Marylander 119

IV. The Evolution of the Medieval Country House in Maryland . . . 121

V. The Maryland Cross-Dwelling 134

VI. Crossroads Churches and Meetinghouses 139

VII. The Persistence of the Medieval Style into the Nineteenth Century . 145

VIII. A Summary of the Maryland Style 158

PART IV

MEDIEVAL ARCHITECTURE OF THE DEEP SOUTH

I. Bermuda 167

II. North Carolina 172

III. South Carolina 177

IV. Georgia 183

Bibliography 187

Index 193

Illustrations

VIRGINIA

Medieval Types of Construction Employed Before 1620 in Virginia . . . 11
Diagram Showing the English Medieval Period of Architecture 14
Medieval Chimneys and Wattling; Jamestown Guest House 19
The Medieval Town House in Virginia and England 23
The Block of Five Houses at Jamestown 31
Casements and Latches from Virginia and England 33
Medieval Door and Furniture Hardware from Jamestown 34
Side Chimneys, Barred Windows, and Ingle Recesses 39
Comparative Virginian and English House Plans 41
Medieval Brick Houses of Virginia and England 45
Pinewoods, or Warburton House, in James City County, Virginia . . . 46
The Triple "Diamond" Stacks of Bacon's Castle 47
More Medieval Types of Virginia Dwellings 49
Medieval Double-Parlor Houses and a Virginia Plot Plan 53
Bacon's Castle, Surry County, Virginia, c. 1650 55
Jacobean Gables in Virginia and England 57
Gothic Chimneys in Virginia and England 61
Embryonic Classic Pediments; Black Diapering 63
Two Medieval Cross-Houses in Virginia 67
Medieval Battlemented Doorways in Virginia and England 69
Christ's Cross, or Criss Cross 70
The Tudor Doorway at Christ's Cross, New Kent County, Virginia . . . 71
Medieval Cross-Plans in Virginia 75
Carved Woodwork, Christ's Cross, Virginia 77
Another Virginia Cross-House and Some Medieval Curtains 79
The Gothic "Old Brick Church," or St. Luke's, Isle of Wight County, Virginia 80
Medieval Churches in Virginia and England 83
Malvern Hill, Henrico County, Virginia 84
The Persistence of the Medieval Style in Eighteenth-Century Virginia . . 89
More Dwellings of Medieval Style in Eighteenth-Century Virginia . . . 93

The Persistence of the Medieval Style in Eighteenth- and Nineteenth-Century
    Virginia 95
Towles Point, Lancaster County, Virginia 104
Gunn's Run, Charles City County, Virginia 104

MARYLAND

The Brick State House of 1676, St. Mary's City, Maryland 105
The Governor's Castle, St. Mary's City, Maryland, 1639 109
Castle and Cottage in Earliest Maryland 111
Medieval Town Houses in Maryland, and Comparative Country House Plans
    Showing Development 117
Medieval Maryland Dwellings 123
More Medieval Maryland Dwellings 125
The Jacobean Influence in Maryland and England 131
Medieval Cross-Houses in Maryland and England 133
Old Bond Castle in Maryland 137
The Dining Room of Bond Castle 138
Trinity Church, Dorchester County, Maryland, c. 1680 139
Medieval Wainscoting in Maryland and England 141
Crossroads Churches and Meetinghouses of Maryland 143
The Transition in Maryland Architecture 149
The Persistence of the Medieval Style in Eighteenth-Century Maryland . . 153
More Medieval Dwellings in Eighteenth- and Nineteenth-Century Maryland 155
More Medieval Dwellings in Later Maryland; Chimneys in England and
    Maryland 161
Holly Hill, Anne Arundel County, Maryland 162
The Original Holly Hill (c. 1667) 163

BERMUDA, THE CAROLINAS, GEORGIA

Bermuda Architecture of Medieval Style 169
The Medieval Style in North Carolina 175
The Medieval and Jacobean Styles in South Carolina 179
The Persistence of Medieval Style in Nineteenth-Century Georgia . . . 181
The White-Newbold House, Near Hertford, Perquimans County, North Caro-
    lina 182
The Thornton House, Green County, Georgia 183

FOREWORD

I T IS seldom that a medievalist finds himself among familiar surroundings in the American scene, but in this volume Dr. Forman has produced a wealth of convincing and intriguing evidence that the beginnings of home- and church-building in Virginia, Maryland, and elsewhere in the South were rooted in English late Gothic usage. From such sources come, for one thing, the quaint terms that have occasionally lingered on the tongues of present day American carpenters and builders. "Intriguing" is a word suggested by Dr. Forman's drawings and what he has to say about them.

In this book on early American architecture we get not only a clear conception of the evolution from the story-and-attic, one-room-deep house, through the house with central hallway, to the cross-plan dwelling with porch in front and staircase at the rear, but also a great deal about the first and very primitive homemaking that was done on these shores. By way of contrast are the Georgian mansions, the usual theme of the historian of colonial architecture, which, as Dr. Forman shows, were products of a later and far more prosperous period. The names which the early settlers gave to their simple homesteads — Kis Kis Kiack, Sweet Hall, Pinewoods, Christ's Cross (shortened to Criss Cross), Brick Billy, Greenway, Resurrection Manor, The Ending of Controversie — show that their construction was a labor of love and that "home" in those days at least was a destination, not a point of departure such as it has of late become. These colonists chose their building forms from those that they remembered in the England which they had left behind — modest models clinging to medieval practice, and made more modest still by the narrow facilities which the New World afforded.

The Architecture of the Old South incorporates lectures given recently at Goucher College, along with the results of a great deal of field experience in archaeology with the United States Department of the Interior. Of extraordinary value is the appearance in these pages of many previously unpublished examples and new data, which is to be attributed chiefly to Dr. Forman's exceptional access to sources while he was serving as editor of the Historic American Buildings Survey in the Fine Arts Division of the Library of Congress. The author is at present professor and department head of art and archaeology at Agnes Scott College.

CHARLES RUFUS MOREY

Princeton University

ACKNOWLEDGMENTS

Grateful acknowledgments are here expressed to Mr. Talbot Hamlin of Columbia University; Mr. Samuel Eliot Morison of Harvard University; and Mr. Robert L. Wiggins of Wesleyan College, Macon, Georgia, for their constructive criticisms of the manuscript.

With her literary skill the late Elizabeth Chandlee Forman, of Haverford, Pennsylvania, assisted in many details of the text.

Thanks in particular are owing to the University Center in Georgia for a grant-in-aid toward the publication of this volume.

NOTE ON THE ILLUSTRATIONS

Where no source is noted, it is to be understood that the illustration was derived from the author's own notes or photographs taken at the site.

Figs. 1–7 appeared in the College Art Journal, vol. VI, no. 2; Fig. 23 in the author's *Jamestown and St. Mary's* (1938); Fig. 30 in *Antiques* for January, 1941; and Fig. 110 is from an engraving in *Battles and Leaders of the Civil War*, vol. 2 (1887).

Fig. 52 is used by courtesy of the Williamsburg Restoration, Inc.; Fig. 145, by courtesy of Mr. James R. Edmunds, Jr.; Fig. 186, after a water color by Mrs. A. L. Sioussat, by permission; Fig. 249, by the kindness of Capt. and Mrs. H. P. LeClair (1942); Fig. 282, by courtesy of Mr. E. V. Jones. Figs. 53, 92, 109, 146, and 281 are from the files of the Historic American Buildings Survey (HABS) in the Library of Congress.

H. C. F.

Bond Castle, Maryland, speaks eloquently of the forces which created American civilization, for it was a bit of English medievalism expressed in the American medium of timber and plank.

WERTENBAKER, *The Founding of American Civilization.*

PART I

Our English Gothic Heritage

I

THE FIELD OF THE CLOTH OF GOLD

THE story of the medieval period in American architecture commences about 1520, the year when King Henry VIII of England paid a visit to Francis I of France, and ends about 1702, the year when Queen Anne ascended the English throne. This interval, therefore, covers almost two centuries, the sixteenth and the seventeenth, in which American architecture was essentially medieval, and largely English at that. This true medieval period in America should not be confused with that nineteenth-century pseudo-medievalism, the Gothic Revival, which introduced a false style of the Middle Ages.

It seems self-evident that American architecture by and large is literally English at its roots, because the United States of America sprang from the thirteen English colonies on the Atlantic seaboard. Properly speaking, Dutch, French, Swedish, and Spanish architecture was an intrusion in the English architecture of the Colonies; not a single one of these "foreign" styles waxed to preponderance in the blossomtime of these provinces. Further, the principal inheritance of the Old South was English;[1] and if any section of the coast had a nearly pure English architecture at this period, it was in the region south of the Mason and Dixon line.

Now when Henry VIII, as the guest of the French king, made his cross-channel excursion to the Field of the Cloth of Gold, he and his courtiers, while there, absorbed a little of French Renaissance culture; consequently they returned to England with something more than full stomachs and weighty gifts. To an island which up to that time knew little but a strong, isolated medievalism, the English monarch carried the seeds of the classical Renaissance. Nonetheless, it should be marked well that it was a very long time before those seeds flourished throughout the length and breadth of England.

In truth, English architecture from 1520 until far into the seventeenth century was not classical, but medieval. The textbooks — and on them the art historian and student generally rely — declare that the end of the medieval period in English architecture coincided with the accession of Elizabeth in 1558;[2] that the Early Renais-

[1] Wertenbaker (1942), p. 1.
[2] Fletcher (1924), p. 701.

sance style, comprising Elizabethan (1558-1603) and Jacobean (1603-1625), then came to the English scene, followed by the High Renaissance of the Anglo-Classic (1625-1702) and the Georgian (1702-1850). These nomenclatures of style are purely arbitrary, and help to conceal the fact of the overpowering persistence of medieval building traditions in England. As has been indicated, until far into the seventeenth century — indeed, almost to the year 1700 — most British structures were erected in the fashion of the Middle Ages.

Even so, how may the persistence of medieval style be explained, especially since Inigo Jones had brought Palladio's books on architecture home from Italy by 1615 and finished the pilastered Banqueting House at Whitehall in London as early as 1622, at the very threshold of the High Renaissance? The answer is that for nearly two hundred years after the Field of the Cloth of Gold the Renaissance did not agree with the average Britisher. He relished his Gothic heritage; and like his tea today, he would not give it up.

Consequently there was no immediate blossoming of the Renaissance after the Field of the Cloth of Gold: the coming of the new manner was gradual; the passing of the old was slow.[3] It is not generally realized that, even after the Renaissance began "knocking at the door, in many places it knocked in vain."[4] In the sixteenth century, most English buildings had no glass for their windows, whereas Renaissance architecture is predicated on glass windows. In the sixteenth century, most British structures had no doors for their doorways, but only claddings,[5] tapestries, or leather hangings to keep out the weather, whereas Renaissance architecture emphasizes the door.

It is true that in certain regions of England the new continental, classical ideas are known to have invaded the domain of some rich burghers and aristocrats, and to have swept away Gothic architecture in certain high places; but what is a drop in a bucket? Far into the seventeenth century, practically all the remaining domestic architecture continued to be built in the traditional manner of the Middle Ages.[6] Elizabethan architects in the sixteenth century had adhered to the late Gothic plan for smaller houses,[7] and the lofty medieval hall with central hearth remained popular through the greater part of that century.[8] In the succeeding hundred years, the typical large country houses of the north and west of England, like those of Yorkshire, followed

---

[3] Lloyd (1931), p. 62.
[4] Simpson (1922), III, 228.
[5] Curtains.
[6] Lloyd (1931), p. 62.
[7] Fletcher (1924), pp. 708, 710, 713.
[8] Braun (1940), p. 59.

the twelfth-century arrangement of central "house," with thalamus or bower on one side and "hall" on the other.[9] And if you had visited England at the beginning of the eighteenth century, when good Queen Anne began her reign, you would have seen that the majority of the rural farmhouses everywhere were in effect medieval buildings, only one room in thickness.

Since the larger part of English buildings continued in the traditional manner until close to 1700, it is not surprising that American architecture in the first century of permanent settlement was likewise medieval. This fact is even less astonishing when the lag in American constructional methods is taken into account. In the seventeenth century it required a long time for a style to cross an ocean. On the Atlantic seaboard there was a lagging averaging about fifty years behind the style in England. Consequently, American architecture was even more medieval than the coeval English manner.

It is our premise, which this volume bears out, that en bloc American architecture of the Southern Colonies in the sixteenth and seventeenth centuries belonged to the English medieval period, which, far from terminating with the accession of Elizabeth, continued until close to 1700 (Fig. 8). Distance did not dilute or corrupt the style in America. The lag only brought it closer to the heart of medievalism.

At all events, it seems prophetic that, in spite of Renaissance influences imbibed on the Field of the Cloth of Gold, the English king, as is a matter of record, continued to carry his Gothic lattice casements from castle to castle as so much household baggage. At the other extremity of the social scale in the British Isles, medievalism remained almost unchanged. For example, in the village of Ballitore, Ireland, in the year 1769, all the parlors, except those at the "Great House" and two other buildings, had earthen floors; the hall doors opened with iron latches; and most of the windows were casements — prime indications of Gothic.[10] Such archaic conditions, strange to relate, prevailed only seven years before the American Revolutionary War.

---

[9] Oswald (1935), p. xviii; Addy (1933), p. 133; Ambler (1913), p. 8.
[10] Leadbeater (1862), I, 72.

II

BEFORE THE CURTAIN ROSE AT JAMESTOWN

NEARLY a century before the founding in 1607 of the permanent colony at Jamestown, the English medieval style of architecture was beginning to infiltrate along the shores of North America, and to set the stage for the medieval period in American architecture.[1] It is true that there is no known record of the appearance of the huts and storehouses which English fishermen built at least as early as 1517 on the coast of Newfoundland, and perhaps Maine as well, but, if these structures were erected in any "style" at all, they must have been, of necessity, medieval constructions. If proof is needed, we can take a look at the Roanoke settlement of 1585 and the St. George's Fort of 1607.

The tragic "City of Raleigh" at Roanoke Island, now in North Carolina, was founded in 1585 by Sir Walter Raleigh. It possessed medievally-fashioned palisaded walls of vertical timbers, and a moat. Its cottages, described as "respectable and necessary," had thatched roofs, dirt floors, and walls probably made of wattles,[2] timber-framing, or brick. There were no log houses at Roanoke.[3]

Until the landing of the Pilgrim Fathers, the region later known as New England was the northern part of Virginia, assigned to the Bristol section of the Virginia Company. Contemporaneously with the founding of Jamestown in *South* Virginia, a fortified outpost by the name of St. George's Fort was entrenched near the mouth of the Kennebec River in Maine, then North Virginia. According to the drawn records of this settlement, a high stone wall, medievally crenelated, encircled the fortification, and a drawbridge extended across a capacious moat. Within the enclosure the buildings, it seems, were constructed of medieval half-timber work, with some kind of filling, like wattles, between the posts. Planks on the roofs appear to have held thatch or swamp sedge in position.

Already the first currents of a medievalism in its last English century, the seventeenth, were beating on these shores when the curtain opened at historic Jamestown.

---

[1] This chapter is based on Forman (1938), chapter i.

[2] A basket work of twigs and branches, plastered over with clay.

[3] Shurtleff in his *Log Cabin Myth* (1939) proves beyond a doubt that there were no log structures at Roanoke and Jamestown.

PART II

Virginia Medieval Architecture

I

THE BEGINNING OF AMERICAN ARCHITECTURE

THE history of American architecture commences on May 14, 1607, with the bivouacking of Edward Maria Wingfield, first president of the King's Council for Virginia, and his companions among the malarial swamps of Jamestown Island. From that day when, unknowingly, they founded the first permanent English settlement in the United States, until Christmas Day, 1620, thirteen years later, when the Pilgrim Fathers began to erect their first house at Plymouth, American architecture was as fundamentally medieval as the ancient churches of the Anglo-Saxons. In truth, it is no exaggeration to compare the earliest Jamestown buildings with those of the Anglo-Saxons, because many were fashioned, *ipso facto*, in the manner of those people of a thousand years before.

The early fabrics, roughly put together among the Jamestown marshes, represent the first chapter in the history of the architecture of the United States; as such, they should be familiar to students of American art and history. The enlarged conception of history now in vogue precludes any indifference on the part of scholars of American history to matters which were of such vital importance to the early founders of this country as the form and construction of their dwellings.[1] When the "ancient planters" established James Fort, as their settlement was called, on a promontory of the Island of Jamestown, and raised other settlements on James River and Eastern Shore, they had recourse to *at least* five different types of English medieval architecture. The names of these kinds of construction are the palisade, the puncheon, the cruck, timber-framing, and part-brick-and-part-framing. No buildings at Jamestown were log cabins, as has been definitely proven in recent years.

Undoubtedly the palisade or stockade was the first type of medieval architecture employed in the land of Virginia. It was used at Jamestown in 1607, and from then until the abandonment of the city in 1699 as the colonial capital. We find that the small fort at Old Point Comfort (1609), the town walls of Henrico or Henricopolis (1611), and the first church on the Eastern Shore of Virginia were constructed by this method. That the palisade was common throughout the countryside is indicated by

[1] Professor Samuel E. Morison points this out in Shurtleff (1939), p. 7.

MEDIEVAL TYPES OF CONSTRUCTION EMPLOYED BEFORE 1620 IN VIRGINIA

1. Church of St. Andrew, Greenstead, Essex, England, c. 1013, showing Anglo-Saxon palisades. (After *Essex*, II)

2. A puncheoned cottage with wattle-and-daub filling, Virginia, 1619. (Conjectural reconstruction)

3. A cruck house near Tewkesbury, Gloucestershire, England. (After Braun, 1940)

4. Cruck church, Jamestown, Virginia, 1607. (Conjectural reconstruction)

5. Timber-framed, one-bay cottage, Colemere, Shropshire, England, late seventeenth century. (After Braun, 1940)

6. Bostall Farm, Woolwich, near London, late sixteenth or early seventeenth century, showing part-brick-and-part-frame construction. (After *London*, V)

7. A "faire row" of framed houses, Jamestown, Virginia, 1611, illustrating five types of timber-framing most commonly used about 1600 in England. Left to right: half-timber work with brick filling; plaster; weatherboarding or clapboards; half-timber-work with plaster; tile-hung. (Conjectural reconstruction)

the governmental edicts of 1624 and 1626 "to palisade in" all dwelling houses.[2] This expression means to surround all habitations with stockaded walls about seven and a half feet high, or more.[3] The English called them "Park-pales." In this way each plantation comprised a little fort against Indian depredations.

Noteworthy must have been the appearance of the triangular James Fort, within the "pallizadoes" of which lay the cradle of the United States. The south side faced the muddy James and measured four hundred twenty feet; the other two sides were each three hundred feet long. At the corners rose bulwarks, sometimes called watch-towers or blockhouses, carrying framed platforms with mounted cannon. The chief doorway was in the middle of the south curtain wall, and each bulwark had a gateway as well. A moat or deep trench encircled the entire fortification.

In structure, the palisades of James Fort comprised strong posts and planks embedded four feet deep in the earth, and standing about fourteen feet high. In order that armed guards could swiftly traverse the palisades, there were passages on the inside of the curtains. The bulwarks, made of giant timbers, surmounted these passages.

Another kind of palisade was incorporated in the walls of the first church on the Eastern Shore, built probably in 1623. Vertical posts were set close together and interwoven with wattles or small branches, daubed with clay.[4]

When they resorted to palisades, the founding fathers of old Virginia continued an unbroken custom of their ancestors reaching back in time through the Gothic and Norman eras to the Anglo-Saxon period. It is said that upon the conquest of Britain in the fifth century the Saxons, ignoring the empty Roman villas, set up their own hovels with walls of split tree trunks placed vertically side by side.[5] At the Battle of Hastings, Harold, last of the Saxon kings, entrenched himself behind deep ditches and "artful" palisades. At any rate, the palisade is the oldest form of wooden construction know today in England, and is derived from paleolithic Europe.[6]

Fortunately for the antiquarian, one Anglo-Saxon wooden building remains. The nave of the little parish church of St. Andrew at Greenstead-by-Ongar, Essex, England (Fig. 1), is probably the timber chapel built about 1013 to commemorate the passing of St. Edmund's body through the town of Ongar.[7] The walls are of split oak timbers set upright on a modern sill.

The second medieval type of construction employed in Virginia is much like the first. This method is building with puncheons, sometimes called "punches" or "quar-

[2] Kingsbury (1933), III, 209.
[3] Minutes of Council, pp. 109, 120, 479.
[4] Mason (1940).
[5] Trevelyan (1926), pp. 39, 149.
[6] Addy (1910), p. 4.
[7] Essex, II, 112.

ters." We find them in 1619 at Berkeley on James River. In this small town there were certain houses merely "covered with boards," which were so inflammable that one firebrand would have been enough to touch them off. Other dwellings were "only made of wood," and had "punches sett into the Ground." Now, in medieval England, puncheons were upright timbers set into the earth, so that the space between them was about equal to the width of the timber itself (Figs. 2, 12). That is, if the timber was twelve inches wide, then the distance between two timbers was likewise twelve. Another name for this method is "post and pan," where the post is the same size as the panel. Usually the intervening spaces were filled with wattle-and-daub. Wattles comprise a basket work of hazel bands fastened between the upright timbers, which were grooved for the purpose. Then the wattles were daubed on both sides with a plaster made of lime and loam mixed with chopped straw. This method was prevalent in Surrey, England; [8] and the Virginia procedure must have been much the same. Actually, puncheoning was nothing but a pseudo-palisading.

Captain John Smith, who for so long endeavored to take more than his share of credit for the Virginia enterprise, introduces us to the third medieval type of structure in Virginia. The colonists, he declares, for their church of 1607 "built a homely thing like a barne, set upon Cratchets, covered with raftes, sedge and earth" (Fig. 4). He also notes that the walls were covered with the same materials, and that the best of the houses were of like curiosity.[9] The *Oxford English Dictionary* reveals that the word "cratchet" is a seventeenth-century variation of "crotchet" or "crotch," meaning a forked pole to support the ridgepole of a dwelling. The writer agrees with Professor Morison [10] in his belief that Smith, writing of cratchets, was thinking of "crucks." To be specific, the cruck was a later, fourteenth-century development of the crotchet and comprised, not a forked pole, but a pair of bent or curved tree trunks placed together in the form of a Gothic arch. In fact by 1600 the English had all but discarded the crotchet and were using the cruck method.[11] It is logical to believe that the Jamestonians employed the fourteenth-century cruck, rather than the earlier crotchet. For all that, both were purely medieval.

In England cottages still stand on crucks after four hundred years. In the middle of Elizabeth's reign a survey made of the village of Crakehon in northern England indicated that every house and barn stood upon "crocks" and was covered with thatch. Today random examples of existing crucks (Fig. 3) may be mentioned: the fourteenth-century manor houses of Oldcourt Farm, Longtown; Ty-Mawr; and Wood House Farm, Ledbury — all of Herefordshire; or sixteenth-century Daren Farm barn, Llan-

[8] Green (1908), p. 30.

[9] Smith (1884), p. 957.

[10] Shurtleff (1939), p. 138, n. 25.

[11] Addy (1910), pp. 39, 40.

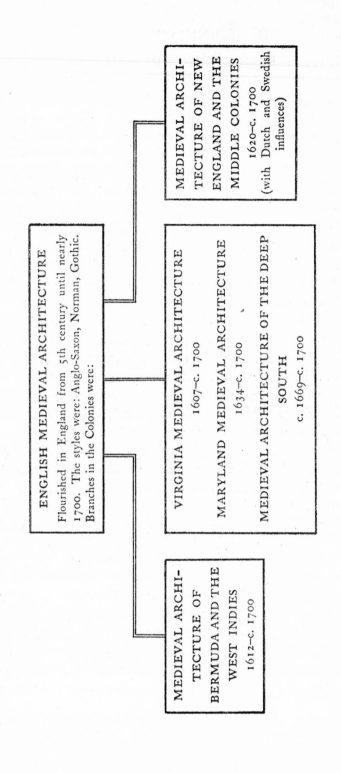

ENGLISH MEDIEVAL ARCHITECTURE

Flourished in England from 5th century until nearly 1700. The styles were: Anglo-Saxon, Norman, Gothic. Branches in the Colonies were:

MEDIEVAL ARCHITECTURE OF NEW ENGLAND AND THE MIDDLE COLONIES
1620–c. 1700
(with Dutch and Swedish influences)

VIRGINIA MEDIEVAL ARCHITECTURE
1607–c. 1700

MARYLAND MEDIEVAL ARCHITECTURE
1634–c. 1700

MEDIEVAL ARCHITECTURE OF THE DEEP SOUTH
c. 1669–c. 1700

MEDIEVAL ARCHITECTURE OF BERMUDA AND THE WEST INDIES
1612–c. 1700

8. DIAGRAM SHOWING THE ENGLISH MEDIEVAL PERIOD OF ARCHITECTURE

veynol, in the same shire; or the seventeenth-century dwellings at Hemington, Leicestershire, and Colemere, Shropshire.[12] These are a few specimens in a country where,
until the year 1700, houses built upon crucks dotted the landscape, especially in the
west and north.[13]

The simplest English dwelling, one bay, or compartment, in length, comprised two
pairs of bent tree trunks, in shape like the lancet arches of a Gothic cathedral, set upon
the ground, strengthened by tie beams, and fastened by wooden pegs. There is a clear
analogy between the cathedral, with its arches and series of bays, and the cruck house,
also with pointed arches and bays. It is a coincidence, perhaps, that the curved shape
of a cruck structure appeared like the inverted hull of a ship, and the word nave, like
the nave of a cathedral, is derived from the Latin, *navis*, ship. The whole genealogy
of the cruck has a strong medieval flavor.

In conjunction with the medieval bay there is an interesting story. This unit of
space measured about sixteen feet, because that was the room needed to house two pairs
of oxen. Whereas the ox house, called the "shippon," a term perhaps reminiscent of
the ship-shape of the cruck building, was often under the same roof as the dwelling,
the practice developed in medieval England of making of uniform length all the bays
under the same roof. The adoption of a standard unit helped the real estate dealers of
the Middle Ages, who could advertise, for instance, that Oldcourt Farm comprised
four bays — a four-bay manor. When a twelve-bay manor was purchased, one knew
how long it was without further description.

At James Fort the number of bays in church and other fabrics was limited by the
known size of the palisade. It would appear that owing to lack of elbowroom the
church of 1607 could not have been more than four bays, or about sixty-four feet.[14]
Lord Delaware's later church, of 1610, measured only sixty feet by twenty-four. In
addition, at James Fort the rows of dwellings, or streets of "settled houses," could
not have been more than ten bays each, along two sides of the palisade. At the very
most the river-front side could not have had more than fourteen bays. Accordingly, it
is possible that in 1607 Jamestown had about thirty-four row lodgings, each about
sixteen feet square. And the best of these were cruck buildings.

Another feature of the Middle Ages that these primitive structures usually possessed was the thatched roof, bound and reeded as in old England. When James City
burned on January 4, 1608, the fire spread easily from one thatched roof to another.
All but three cabins were consumed like paper. It is surmised that something more

[12] *Herefordshire*, I, 185, 186; II, 116; III, pl. 36.
[13] Braun (1940), p. 66.
[14] Forman (1938), p. 39.

than wooden chimneys caused this conflagration: there were Spanish spies at Jamestown.

The old English word "timbran" meant "to timber," or "to build." [15] Timber-
framing, the next logical step in the development of puncheon and cruck, is the fourth
medieval type of architecture known in earliest Virginia. As the great timber forests
of England began to dwindle, it was discovered that the vertical posts in a house need
not be placed close together, as in puncheoning, but could be widely spaced and re-
inforced by diagonal braces. Such buildings became known as timber-framed (Fig. 5),
where the posts, studs, and sills were tied together with wooden pegs. In the case of
the cruck building, the outside walls were built up with widely spaced timbers, to the
extent that the crucks could be taken away altogether, leaving a timber-framed house.

The town of Berkeley on the James had, besides puncheoned dwellings, two structures which were mentioned in 1619 as being timber-framed. Virginians called them
"English houses" or "fair houses." The swing of the English to timber-framing in
the latter part of the sixteenth century [16] — although, of course, the constructional
method was not then new — is reflected in the Jamestown of 1611, which had "two
faire rows of howses, all of framed Timber, two stories, and an upper Garret, or Corne
loft high." Also in Virginia, at Henricopolis there were in 1611 "3 streets of well
framed houses"; at Rocke Hall, "a faire framed parsonage"; and at Bermuda City,
"very faire houses." [17] Although always to remain "castles in the air," the guest houses
or inns (Figs. 14, 15) ordered in 1620 by the Virginia Company of London were
likewise to be timber-framed, in the following manner: "Each Plantation shall each
of them build, at their common charge, labour and industry, frame, build and perfect
. . . a guest house, for the lodging and entertaining of fifty persons in each, upon
their first arrival." [18] Each housing was to be one hundred eighty feet in length and
sixteen wide, or, in other words, roughly ten bays. At suitable locations five chimneys
were to be erected, and windows were to be well placed for ventilation. A bit of local
color was added to the instructions in the specification that each guest house was to
contain twenty-five bedsteads, four feet by six, standing two feet from the ground,
with board partitions between them. The use of earth as floor recalls certain medieval
halls where dirt was covered with rushes.

Not only did the art of timber-framing comprise the setting up of upright posts at
some distance apart, the tenoning of them into a sill at the bottom and a wall-plate at
the top, but it also included the filling between, or covering over, the posts. The fact
that one kind of filling was common in this period in Virginia is certain from William

[15] Addy (1910), p. 106.
[16] Lloyd (1931), p. 7.
[17] Hamor (1615), pp. 30, 31, 33.
[18] Kingsbury (1933), III, 267.

Strachey's reference (1610-11) to buildings which were "pargetted and plaistered with Bitumen [a kind of asphalt] or tough clay." [19] As already noted, this is the wattle-and-daub method (Fig. 13), oldest known technique of filling interstitial spaces in England.

Since Virginia summers are hot, such wattle panels in timber-framed dwellings heated up "like Stoves"; and it seems likely that wattle-and-daubing was soon discarded for better types of insulation. In England at the time, several other fillings or coverings for timber-framed houses were in vogue, such as: brick nogging, laid either horizontally or in herringbone fashion; ordinary plaster; shingle tiles hung from battens nailed across the posts; or weatherboards (clapboards). Since all these materials were manufactured in Virginia in 1611, timber-framed buildings could have been constructed with any of them (Fig 7).

In the weatherboarded dwelling it was customary to fill in with an insulating material just as today we pump our walls full of rock-wool. On the James, mud, brick or coarse saltmarsh grass could have been employed in the earliest years. This last method, the grass-stuffed wall, was used in 1627 in Massachusetts.[20] Jamestonians, surrounded by seven hundred and fifty acres of island swamps, must have also employed grass.

The last known method of medieval construction in Virginia before 1620 is what may be termed "half-and-half" work, that is, part brick and part timber-framing. In 1611 at Henricopolis, men constructed not only three streets of well-framed dwellings, but also "competent and decent houses, the first storie all of bricks." [21] Of course the "half-and-half" type formed the transition between the timber-framed dwelling and the all-brick. That there were all-brick edifices in Virginia before 1620 we do not know, but, since brick was manufactured at James City from the first, there is that probability. At any rate, the "half-and-half" fabric was an advance over ordinary timber-framing, and the method was common enough in the late medieval period in England (Fig. 6). For example, the manor-house of Saint Aylotts (c. 1500) at Saffron Walden, Essex,[22] is a "House of two storeys: the lower storey is of brick and the upper storey timber-framed and plastered."

[19] Purchas (1906), XIX, 57, 58.
[20] At the Aptuxcet Trading Post.
[21] Johnson (1612).
[22] *Essex*, I, 242.

MEDIEVAL CHIMNEYS AND WATTLING; JAMESTOWN GUEST HOUSE

9. Carmarthen, Wales. A wooden "Welsh" chimney with wattled hood. (After *Wales and Monmouthshire*)

10. Road View Kitchen, New Kent County, Virginia, nineteenth century. Cross section showing wood and plaster chimney. (After HABS)

11. Bacon's Castle, Surry County, Virginia, c. 1650. Hooded brick fireplace in attic.

12. Gainsborough Old Hall, Lincolnshire, England, fifteenth century. Wattles between puncheons. (After Garner and Stratton, 1911)

13. Withington Farm Barn, Kilpeck, England. Wattles exposed in half-timber work. (After *Herefordshire*, I)

14. Almshouse, Friern Barnet, England, c. 1612. Compare with Fig. 15. (After *Middlesex*)

15. Jamestown, Virginia, 1620. Timber-framed guest house. (Conjectural reconstruction)

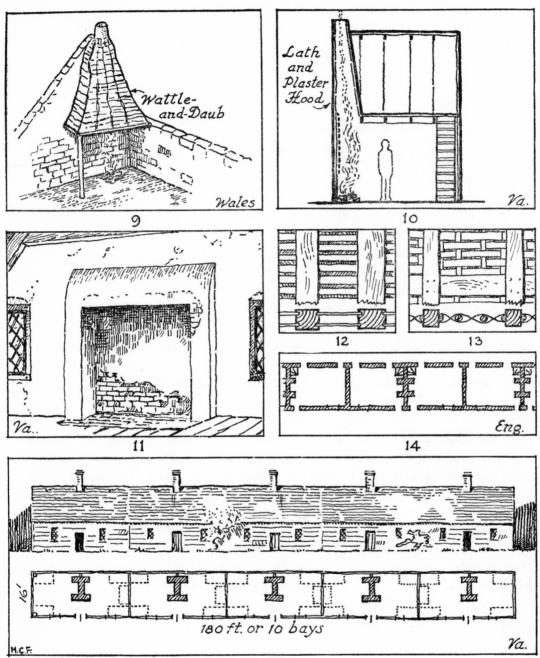

Wattle-
and-Daub

Wales

9

Lath
and
Plaster
Hood

Va.

10

Va.

11

12

13

Eng.

14

16'

180 ft. or 10 bays

Va.

H.C.F.

15

II

A LANDSCAPE OF WOODEN CHIMNEYS

For its first thirteen years Virginia architecture developed everywhere the wooden chimney. So inherently medieval is the wooden chimney, that its ancestry extends back in time to the eleventh century. William Strachey, first secretary of the Virginia colony, when describing the wattled buildings of James City, also called attention to the "wide and large Country chimnies," in which well-wooded fires could be maintained. Now a country chimney in those days signified a fireplace and flue of wood, in contradistinction to a city chimney of masonry. But before Strachey's time, as for example in 1400, practically all British homes, if they possessed them at all, used wooden chimneys. A London ordinance of 1419 declared that no chimney should be made thenceforth unless it was of stone, brick, or plaster, and that all wooden chimneys should be pulled down.[1] What a fire hazard London must have been!

Throughout yeoman England, wooden chimneys seem to have become common only after the latter part of the fourteenth century.[2] Fortunately for students, there are a number of wooden chimneys extant in English houses comprising little more than great hoods. Such hoods or canopies were made of wooden timbers and wattle-and-daub, and were placed to rest on the second story floor. The arrangement worked something like this: the fire was built on the ground floor against the wall, which was covered with a brick or stone backing, known as a reredos.[3] The smoke found its way into the hood on the second story, and thence out a wood or clay stack on the roof. Sometimes the stack was only a barrel with the bottom knocked out.

Since the hood was large in order to catch the smoke, it often projected four or five feet into the upper room. In Westmorland, England, the outbuilding of Scalegate, Askham, built about 1700, has an original timber and plaster hood in a very good state of preservation. Other canopies are at High Birk House, Little Langdale, and Boundary Bank Cottage, Underbarrow, both in Westmorland.[4]

[1] Addy (1910), p. 119.
[2] Sparrow (1909), p. 88.
[3] Braun (1940), p. 78.
[4] *Westmorland*, pp. 24, 33, 149, 231.

Another name for the wooden fireplace and hood is "Welsh chimney," which in Wales, or on the English side of the Welsh border, is a wicker and thatch contraption (Fig. 9). The poles or sticks of the wattled hood generally projected through the thatched roof; and a rounded clay coating was daubed on the sticks to make a stack. Circular stacks like these were regular features of Pembrokeshire dwellings two centuries ago. In England, at a place called Darwin in Lancashire, stands a timber hood constructed of oak posts with short rails placed at intervals and intertwined with branches.[5]

While none of Strachey's country chimneys has been preserved for us, we are particularly fortunate in our knowledge of a wooden chimney extant in Virginia. Near St. Peter's Church, New Kent County, stands a frame, one-story-and-attic outbuilding, by the name of Road View Kitchen (Fig. 10). This little hut represents the survival of a medieval building type existing in the early nineteenth century. One can not state, therefore, that the structure is medieval. The fire was kindled on a dirt floor against a gable-end wall. An iron fireback or reredos was employed; above this protector lath strips, heavily clayed, were nailed to the wall. In the attic floor there is a large lath-and-plaster hood, exactly like the type in England already described. The hood gradually tapers almost to the ridgepole, where it joins a boarded, boxed shaft, projecting only a foot above the ridge. Tradition has it that buckets of water and a ladder were always kept in readiness.

So prevalent in Virginia became the wooden chimney, after Strachey's time, that a gentleman by the name of William Fitzhugh went out of his way to write in 1686 that all the dwellings of his large plantation were furnished with brick chimneys. Further, in 1708, one Littlepage was instructed to build a dwelling (Fig. 116) with lathed and plastered chimneys and with brick hearths and backs. As late as 1750, the wood chimneys of York, Virginia, were ordered to be removed, and new ones forbidden to be erected.

Of course, in England the original manner of laying a fire had been, not against the wall, but in the center of the room. The father of Harold, the Saxon king, lived in a mansion having no less than three rooms where fires could be lit in the middle of the floor.[6] Sometimes there were openings in the roof, called louvers, for the abundant smoke to find its way out. Many ancient Cornish buildings have central hearths with wood-and-plaster hoods suspended from the rafters to catch the smoke. Exactly when the English began to place their wooden hoods against the walls is not known, but in the thirteenth century Henry III ordered a temporary apartment, known as a *cami-*

---

[5] Lloyd (1931), p. 347.
[6] Bulwer Lytton describes this in his novel, *Harold, the Last of the Saxon Kings*, p. 426.

THE MEDIEVAL TOWN HOUSE IN VIRGINIA AND ENGLAND

16. The First State House, Jamestown, Virginia, c. 1635. A reconstruction. (After Forman, 1938)

17. English row gables, Bocking, Essex, England. (After *Essex*, I)

18. First State House, Jamestown, Virginia, c. 1635. Unit floor plan. (Reconstruction)

19. A unit floor plan of a London row house, England, seventeenth century. (After Moxon, 1703)

20. Typical hall-and-parlor dwelling of seventeenth-century England, showing floor plan. (After Braun, 1940)

21. The two Hampton houses, Jamestown, Virginia, seventeenth century. (Conjectural reconstruction)

22. Flax houses, Jamestown, Virginia, 1646. (Conjectural reconstruction)

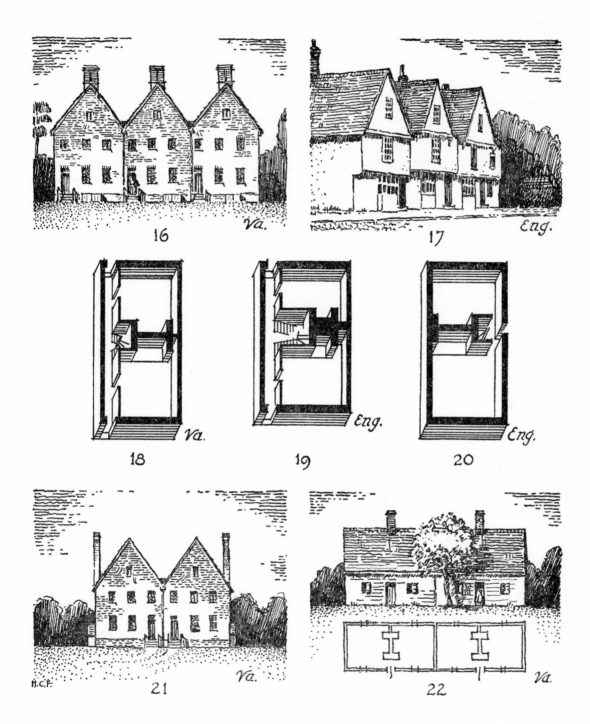

16   *Va.*   17   *Eng.*

18   *Va.*   19   *Eng.*   20   *Eng.*

21   *Va.*   22   *Va.*

natum (from the Latin *caminus*, fireplace), with a plaster chimney and a lean-to roof built against the wall of a tower at Windsor.[7]

At all events, the wooden chimney has a very ancient history in England, and was commonly employed before 1620 in Virginia, and for a long time afterward. We know of one built in New Kent County about one hundred years ago. But originally the landscape was dotted with them, as was medieval England.

[7] Dutton (1935), p. 25; Lloyd (1931), p. 30.

III

THE VIRGINIA HOUSE TRANSPLANTED
FROM ENGLAND

B EFORE the development of Virginia medieval architecture can be outlined,
something about the origins of the English house and its arrangement
should be known. Without this knowledge, it is possible, for example, to
believe that Strachey was being facetious when he wrote of the Virginia
homes of 1610 in the following manner:

> *But Halls we build for us and ours*
> *To dwell in them whilst we live here.*

The expression, "hall," might seem ostentatious in the light of some of the flimsy
and miniature buildings described in previous chapters, unless it is realized that in
Strachey's time the term was synonymous with "house" and was derived from the
chief room in the house.

In actuality "house" means "fire-house," as translated from the Norse, *eld-hús*.
The expression in time came to denote the "house place" or "house-part," the large
room where the master, his family, and servants ate and slept, and where the central
fire was kept.[1] Moreover, the Norse dwelling possessed three apartments: the fire
house, the woman's chamber, and the buttery or pantry. In England of the Middle
Ages the large and medium-sized country seats usually followed this tri-partite division. The floor plan of fourteenth-century Oldcourt Farm, in Herefordshire, shows
this arrangement: "hall," where the central bonfire was maintained; buttery or bottlery
at one end, where food was prepared; and solar or bower, a sunny apartment for
women, at the other. Perhaps the meaning of "hall" is best revealed in the "new
mansion house" of one John Parker of Derbyshire, England, which had in 1632 a
"Hall or Fier-house." [2]

If "hall" seems a grandiose name for a cottage of Virginia pioneers, the title "Great
House" is perhaps an even more elaborate description. This expression also came
from the Old Country. In 1632 James Knott's home in Virginia was "commonly

[1] Addy (1910), p. 82.
[2] *Derb. Arch. Jour.*, V, 45.

called the Great House."[3] And these homes were not large. Christopher Branch of Virginia, who died in the latter half of the seventeenth century, instructed in his will that his son should have a residence twenty feet by sixteen. His own house was smaller by a foot in width. *Mirabile dictu,* his grandson's was only five feet from gable end to gable end. Even the more prominent abodes of the seventeenth century were not large, as we know them. The Green Spring, built about 1646 for Sir William Berkeley, had but six rooms, and it was the largest house of its time in Virginia. The well-known worthy, Thomas Ludwell, resided in a dwelling, dating from the 1650's, which had six rooms, namely: hall, buttery, kitchen, chamber, inner room, and small middle room.

Immediately around the great house, as for example at Bacon's Castle in Virginia (Fig. 61), there were usually strung out long rows of outbuildings, the number of which was dependent upon the size of the plantation. Very prosperous owners possessed dovecots, stables, barns, henhouses, slave quarters, outdoor kitchens, arbors, and dairies. Sometimes there were offices, stores, and schools. A plantation was to all intents and purposes self-sustaining. Nevertheless, it is interesting to find that the Southerner's custom of surrounding himself with dependencies was nothing new, but a characteristic of medievalism. In England the manor house was flanked by outbuildings very similar to those of early Virginia. Oldcourt Farm, already mentioned, has today a cowshed, a cartshed, and two barns.[4] The earlier manor house of Ardleigh, of the twelfth century, containing a hall and adjoining bower, has a kitchen, bakehouse, stable, servant's house, and two storehouses for grain. That the pigeon house was a favorite of early Virginians may be better understood when it is considered that only lords of medieval manors were permitted to keep this kind of bird.

Sometimes it is puzzling why the Southerner often built his kitchen as a separate building. It could only have been an inconvenient arrangement where food had to be carried out of doors to reach the dining room. One may explain the situation by the theory that slaves should be kept at a distance. But the original practice is medieval. The cooking in the manors of England was done out of doors, or in rough shelters or, by the fifteenth century, in separate kitchen buildings with cavernous fireplaces. Meals in the Middle Ages were usually carried across the kitchen courtyard.

The Virginia dwelling of the seventeenth century was much more English than anyone hitherto has supposed. In the writer's opinion the early type of Virginia rural abode was neither "distinctly American" nor "quite unlike" those of the mother country.[5] It was of the English medieval style, sometimes modified by colonial influ-

---

[3] Bruce (1895), II, 151.
[4] *Herefordshire,* I, 184.   [5] Wertenbaker (1942), and Bemis and Burchard (1933), p. 262.

ences. With very few differences, the Virginia house was a transplanted English one.

An interesting coincidence in American history is the fact that the American Indians were employing several types of European medieval construction in their habitations at the time when the earliest white settlers arrived in the southeastern United States. The Indians had acquired these methods independently of European contact: timber-framing with wattle-and-daub panels; thatched roofs; central hearths and louvers in the roof to let out the smoke; palisades and puncheons.[6] Perhaps the English bringing the medieval style to these shores were not so clever, after all? The Indian was smart too, although labeled "savage."

[6] See Bushnell (1919), pp. 32, 34, 56, 58, 64, *et al.*

IV

THE VIRGINIA TOWN HOUSE

IN 1623 the ideal town which the Virginia Company of London had at heart for its tidewater domain on the James River comprised a convenient and suitable number of houses, built together of brick and enclosed with a battlemented brick wall.[1] Never was this desire fulfilled — anywhere. About forty years afterward, in 1662, King Charles of England ordered the General Assembly of Virginia to pass an act for building a town of thirty-two brick houses, set in a square or other form which the governor should choose. His Majesty proposed such a city for every river in Virginia; but the scheme remained a castle in an air antipathetic to bureaucracy.

From the evidence of the Jamestown excavations, the floor plan of the town house conformed to certain stock dimensions in accordance with buildings of medieval England. The size most commonly employed in Virginia was twenty by forty feet, measured on the inside. There were at least three kinds of buildings conforming to this specification. The fact that all three were *row* houses indicates that the English were endeavoring to build a town in the manner of their ancestors. In English minds Jamestown was to be a city of continuous and adjacent habitations, like Oxford and Chipping Camden.

The first variety of twenty-by-forty dwelling is represented by the First State House at Jamestown, now destroyed, but originally one of the most interesting buildings in the country (Figs. 16, 18). It formed three row houses standing along the river bank, of which two were erected before 1635 by Sir John Harvey, and the third before 1655 by Sir William Berkeley. The three units were brick, two stories and "cornloft" high, with gables facing the river on the south and the Back Street on the north.[2]

In his *Mechanick Exercises* Moxon illustrates the plan of a typical London house of the seventeenth century (Fig. 19) which is not very different from the unit plan of the First State House. In fact by changing a few of its dimensions, one could fit the English scheme over the Virginia building.

[1] Kingsbury (1933), IV, 259, 260, 434.
[2] Forman (1938), chapter viii.

In comparing English and Virginia floor plans, the reader may well question why the front and rear walls are thicker than the *party* walls. There was precedent in medieval building laws. In 1189, only a little more than a century after the Norman Conquest, the citizens of London built their homes one story high with party walls three feet thick. The roofs were tile or thatch, and the gables faced the street.[3] By the 1600's, party walls had thinned down to fourteen inches, or, in the old vernacular, one-and-a-half bricks thick. An Act of Parliament ordered that a building fronting on the street should be two stories high besides cellar and garret *when* the front and rear gable walls were two bricks thick and the party walls one-and-a-half bricks thick. These wall thicknesses correspond exactly to those of the First State House in Virginia.

Furthermore, the appearance and details of the First State House were Gothic. There were wrought-iron lattice casements with diamond panes or "quarrels"; English bonded brickwork;[4] and a pantile[5] roof — all features of the medieval house. The front doors had great rim locks over a foot long, with eight-inch keys to match. Inside, the doors were ornamented with ancient types of hinges: the fancy cock's head; the H-hinge with foliated terminations; the strap hinge; the butterfly hinge. There were also ornamental latch locks and latch bars, the designs of which can be almost duplicated in old England (Figs. 28, 29, 30).

The lattice casement, such as filled the window openings of the First State House, has a very interesting origin in Great Britain. In the sixteenth century the use of glass was far from universal, and a casement was rare and costly. In truth, many a window was a "wind hole," rather than a "light hole." Protection from the weather was often obtained by covering the opening with a lattice work made of wicker and fine oak strips, called "calmes." Then oiled paper, linen, or canvas was stretched across the strips. Other windows merely had board shutters with a grillwork of vertical oak or iron bars (Figs. 33, 34). The shutters were placed on the inside of the bars; and the bars themselves, of squarish section, were set on the diagonal in the frame of the window for greater tensile strength. By the early seventeenth century glass became more common in England, and its wider use was reflected in Virginia. Nevertheless, in both places there still must have been plenty of "wind holes" and shutters.

At Jamestown the casements had exactly the same features as those of medieval England (Figs. 25, 26, 27). They had the identical kind of spring latch bars for opening and shutting the window; lead strips or calmes to hold the diamond glass; tiny lead ribbons to tie the calmes to the reinforcing saddle bars; and hinges. Even

---

[3] Addy (1910), chapter vi.
[4] Method of laying bricks by alternate rows of headers and stretchers.
[5] An S-shaped tile about 13 inches long.

the glass had the same greenish cast: it was translucent, not transparent. When Lady Berkeley wished to look through her Virginia windows without being seen by a crowd gathered outside her residence, she had to peek through a broken quarrel. One of the casements from the First State House is only a foot and a half wide — just large enough for a person's shoulders. But there were even smaller casements in early Virginia. On the property of John Washington at Bridges Creek on Potomac River was found a casement only a foot wide (Fig. 24). Bridges Creek, it may be noted, is part of the George Washington Birthplace National Monument; and John Washington, great-grandfather of George, lived there from 1664 until his death in 1677.

Within the First State House at Jamestown were back-to-back fireplaces (Fig. 18), features which arose in England in late medieval times. Then, they were spoken of as the "stack of brick chimneys," standing in the middle of the house. In fourteenth-century Oldcourt Farm, Herefordshire, for example, back-to-back fireplaces were inserted two centuries later in the middle of the hall, dividing it into two rooms. St. Clair's Hall, Essex, has had the same kind of alteration.[6] By the seventeenth century the feature was common all over Britain (Fig. 20). Consequently, it may be inferred that when the English owner became tired of the old smoky bonfire arrangement, he placed a back-to-back fireplace in the same spot. Where the louver crowned the roof to let the smoke out, a stack of chimneys projected.

Row gables facing the street, as illustrated in the First State House, were customary in England from the time of the Anglo-Saxons.[7] One does not have to look far in Britain for the type: Bradford Street, Bocking, Essex (Fig. 17); or the streets of Midhurst, Sussex; or Pinacle Row, Heacham, Norfolk.[8] Even the famous view of London before the Great Fire of 1666 shows how frequent was the "gabled" street.

The second kind of twenty-by-forty house known to Virginia was also a row building; but, unlike the First State House, the gable ends were not on the front. These comprised the long-drawn-out parade of five brick houses, known as the "Country-Ludwell-State House block," [9] situated behind the Brick Church at Jamestown. The fifth structure of this unit, the Third State House, is described later, and need not concern us at the moment. The other four houses, marked on the drawing (Fig. 23) as houses I, II, III, and IV, were probably erected as a result of the bureaucratic act of 1662, setting up thirty-two brick dwellings, each twenty-by-forty within the walls, eighteen feet from floor to eaves, and fifteen feet from eaves to ridge, with roofs of slate or tile. By comparing the floor plan of houses I and II with the unit plan of the First

[6] *Essex*, III, 205.
[7] Braun (1940), p. 17.
[8] *Essex*, I, 37; Dawber (1900), pl. 86.
[9] Forman (1938), pp. 165–168, 171–173.

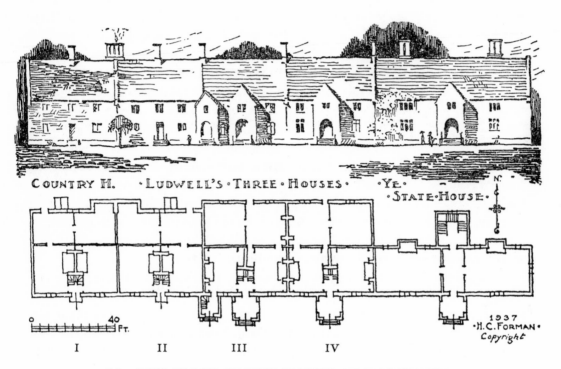

COUNTRY H. ·LUDWELL'S·THREE·HOUSES· ·YE· STATE·HOUSE· N.

I   II   III   IV

1937
·H.C.FORMAN·
Copyright

0   40 FT.

23. THE BLOCK OF FIVE HOUSES AT JAMESTOWN

CASEMENTS AND LATCHES FROM VIRGINIA AND ENGLAND

24. John Washington Farm, Bridges Creek, Westmoreland County, Virginia, c. 1670. Wrought-iron lattice casement, 12¾″ by 18½″.

25. The two Hampton houses, Jamestown, Virginia, seventeenth century. Wrought-iron lattice casement, 13 5/16″ by 25⅛″. (After Forman, 1938)

26. An English casement from Godalming, Surrey, seventeenth century. Size, 13¾″ by 23½″. (After Oliver, 1929)

27. An English casement latch or fastener. (After Holmes, 1915)

28. First State House, Jamestown, Virginia, c. 1635. Wrought-iron latch bar. (After Forman, 1938)

29. An English wrought-iron latch bar and guide, sixteenth century. (After Holmes, 1915)

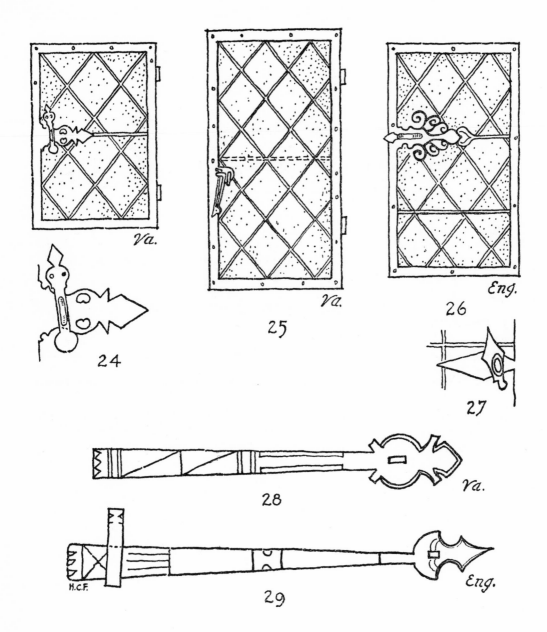

Va.

24

25

Va.

Eng.

26

27

28

Va.

29

Eng.

H.C.F.

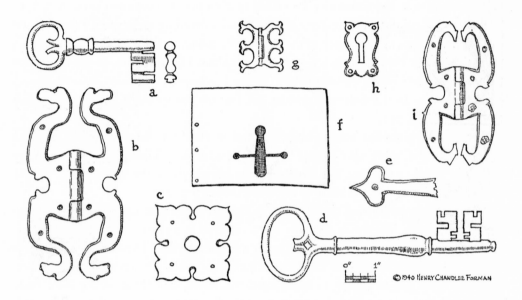

30. MEDIEVAL DOOR AND FURNITURE HARDWARE FROM JAMESTOWN

a, 4″ key; *b*, cock's-head hinge; *c*, door-pull escutcheon; *d*, 8″ key; *e*, part of a strap hinge; *f*, stock-lock main plate; *g*, small brass hinge; *h*, keyhole escutcheon; *i*, cock's-head hinge.

State House (Fig. 18), it will be evident to the reader that the interior arrangement is similar in each case. But a study of the floor plans of houses III and IV reveals, not back-to-back fireplaces, but flush, gable ones.

In addition, it will be noted that two fireplaces at the rear of houses I and II (Fig. 32) were placed on the long sides of the dwellings — the first known example of "side" fireplaces in the Colonies. This kind of chimney was common enough in both Virginia and England. For instance, Holmwood's dwelling at Berkley Plantation in Virginia had (1649) a "chimney at the side of the house on the outside." [10] In Britain we find the same kind of chimney on Little Wenham Hall, Suffolk, of the thirteenth century; Oldcourt Farm, Herefordshire, of the fourteenth; and Saint Aylott's, Essex, of the fifteenth. In the sixteenth century the feature was spread all over the English countryside (Fig. 31).

The two Virginia flax houses, built of wood in 1646 for the manufacture of linen by poor children, were also twenty-by-forty structures.[11] The ceilings were low — only eight feet — and there was a loft of sawn boards above the single story. In the center of each house stood a stack of brick chimneys (Fig. 22).

We need not dwell long on the other stock size of town house: sixteen by twenty-four. Another act, this one in the year 1639, ordered everybody owning five hundred acres to put up a dwelling of this size, with a cellar as well. The two Hampton row houses (Fig. 21), also back of the Brick Church at James City, roughly fit these dimensions. The gables appear to have faced the street, like those of the First State House, and there were leaded casements with diamond panes, handsome wrought-iron hardware, and Delft tiles.

The early Virginia town dwelling was much too confined by medieval building laws to pass through the stages of development undergone by the country house. How could you limit the size of houses by medieval specifications for any great length of time? No city of brick arose at Jamestown. The King's wishes were thwarted; but then, who can blame the Americans?

[10] Blanton (1930), pp. 176, 177.
[11] Hening, I, 336, 337.

V

HOW THE MEDIEVAL COUNTRY HOUSE DEVELOPED

THROUGHOUT the seventeenth century the rural dwelling in Virginia ran a course of development from the simple cottage of one chamber and loft to the great Georgian mansion of the early 1700's. At the same time, it does not necessarily follow that all the most unpretentious dwellings were built first and all the most complex afterward. Some elementary types, beginning early in the seventeenth century, persisted into the succeeding century; nevertheless, the tendency was for the buildings with a relatively large number of rooms to belong almost exclusively to the second half of the seventeenth century. In fact, most of these structures approach the year 1700.

It is odd that most of the town houses in the Virginia of this period were erected two-and-a-half stories high, whereas the country seats, not under building restrictions, were for the most part one story and a half. In England, likewise, the town dwelling was generally more advanced than that of the rural regions. As has been already stated, London had two-story habitations from 1198; but the majority of country abodes were only story-and-loft, until the end of the seventeenth century.

The plainest country dwelling in Virginia is the hut of one bay, or one and a fraction thereof. "Of one bay's breadth, God wot! A silly cote," exclaimed in 1610 the honorable Bishop Hall.[1] The single room of such a contraption included the hall, dining room, and kitchen, all rolled into one; and the loft was just large enough to lie down to sleep in comfortably. Good examples in Virginia were Christopher Branch's cottage, fifteen feet by twenty, and William May's (Fig. 36a), built about 1661 near the Governor's Garden in James City. On the exterior, May's had a central doorway flanked by two little windows, and a chimney at one end. Undoubtedly the cot was of the plainest character.

Still another one-bay dwelling was the wooden "House on Isaac Watson's Land," at Jamestown (Figs. 36, 37), perhaps erected as early as 1644. Here was one twenty-by-twenty room with paved brick floor and a fireplace large enough to take an eight-

---

[1] "Select Poems of Joseph Hall," *Satires*, Book V, Satire I, in Sanford (1819).

foot log. No hovel was this abode, for it had leaded casement windows and elaborate cock's-head hinges. The loft, probably gained by a stepladder, was no doubt big enough for a few small beds. Then there were some odds and ends, like a setting for a brewing copper [2] and a Dutch oven. Flanking either side of the great chimney were probably ingle recesses or chimney pents.

It is interesting to know that such small projecting recesses or closets, less than one bay in length, were known in provincial England and Scotland as "outshuts." [3] An outshut was any "excrescence" or "wart" attached to a building; and one does not have to look far in Britain before finding an example. In a medieval, thatched, one-bay hut set on crucks at Westward in Lancashire, there is a buttery outshut measuring ten-by-four. But when an outshut adjoins a chimney, the English favor the words "ingle recess" or "roofed ingle." [4] The writer's coined expression, "chimney pent," is also descriptive. [5] Sussex and Surrey especially abound in fine chimneys flanked by large ingle recesses, lighted by miniature windows (Fig. 35). Sometimes the oven is a roofed ingle all to itself, forming a picturesque motif, exactly like that of the Watson cottage in James City. Sometimes the ingle recesses come two stories high: Gainsborough Old Hall, a fifteenth-century Lincolnshire mansion, has a whole row of them on its kitchen wing.

The one-bay lodging, like May's and Watson's at Jamestown, has its counterpart in England. Especially reminiscent of May's is the stone cottage at Iccomb in Gloucestershire (Fig. 38), where the chimney is flush with the gable end, and the doorway is centrally located. Another example is a cot near Blackheath, Surrey, with Dutch oven, great fireplace containing seats, large cupboard, and winding staircase. [6]

When the "ancient planter" in Virginia discovered that he possessed a little more means than the one-bay settler, he would erect a new "hall-and-parlor" house, or simply add a parlor to his old "hall." After all, family and furniture will increase.

The hall-and-parlor dwelling, sometimes known as "hall-and-bower," [7] marked the second stage in the development of rural Virginia architecture. In England it was a common *sixteenth-century* type (Fig. 40), with a gable-end chimney or one on the side. A perfect British example is the stone cottage at Tunley (Fig. 159), near Sapperton, Gloucestershire. An old English deed of 1579 describes a hall-and-parlor cottage as "containing two bays of sawn timber . . . to be thatched or clayed." Fortunately, in

[2] Brick compartment with fire door at pavement level.
[3] Addy (1910), chapter 3.
[4] Dawber (1905), p. 17; Clarke (1923), II, xxi.
[5] Forman (1934), p. 23.
[6] Nevill (1889), p. 10; Braun (1940), p. 66.
[7] Addy (1910), p. 133.

SIDE CHIMNEYS, BARRED WINDOWS, AND INGLE RECESSES

31. Broadhurst, Sussex, England, sixteenth century. Side chimneys. (After Wolseley, 1925)

32. Houses I and II, Jamestown, Virginia, c. 1662. Side chimney. (Reconstruction)

33. House at Benenden, Kent, England, fifteenth century. Unglazed window with square oak bars set diagonally in frame. (After Lloyd, 1931)

34. Bacon's Castle, Surry County, Virginia, c. 1650 (left), and Ampthill, Chesterfield County, Virginia, c. 1732 (right). Unglazed cellar windows with square bars set diagonally in frame. Compare with Fig. 33.

35. Cottage, Docklow, Herefordshire, England, late fourteenth-century origin, showing ingle recesses or chimney pents. (After *Herefordshire*, III)

36. One-bay "House on Isaac Watson's Land," Jamestown, Virginia, c. 1644 (?), showing ingle recesses. Reconstruction. (After Forman, 1938)

36a. William May's House, Jamestown, c. 1661. (After Ambler MSS)

31   Eng.

32   Va.

33   Eng.

34   Va.

35   Eng.

36a   36   Va.

H.C.F.

COMPARATIVE VIRGINIAN AND ENGLISH HOUSE PLANS

37. One-bay wooden "House on Isaac Watson's Land," Jamestown, Virginia, c. 1644 (?). Compare with Fig. 36. (After Forman, 1938)

38. Stone cottage at Iccomb, Gloucestershire, England. (After Dawber, 1905)

39. The brick Wishart House, Norfolk, Virginia, c. 1680. Example of hall-and-parlor type. (After HABS)

40. A common type of hall-and-parlor house, with end chimney, in sixteenth-century England. (After Braun, 1940)

41. "House on the Lands of Mr. John Watson and Mr. Knight," Jamestown, Virginia, before 1700. Reconstruction. (After Forman, 1938)

42. Latchley's Manor House, Steeple Bumpstead, Essex, England, c. 1500. (After *Essex*, I)

43. Malvern Hill, Henrico County, Virginia, c. 1662. Example of a cross-house.

44. Chantmarle Manor House, Dorset, England, c. 1604. (After Garner and Stratton, I)

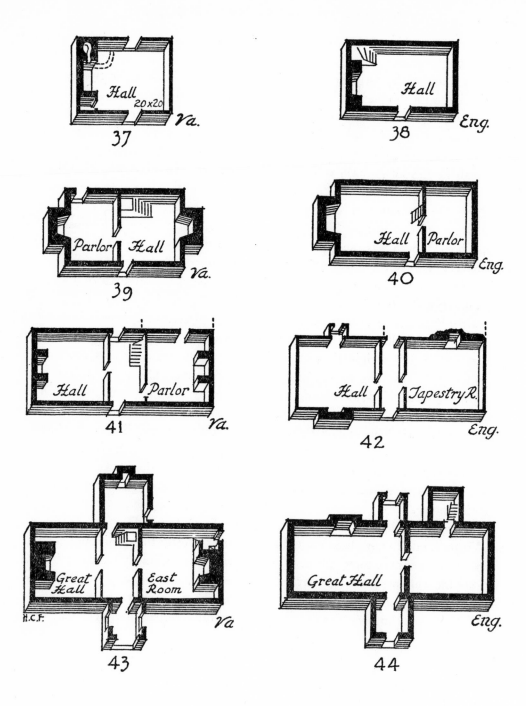

37   Hall 20x20   Va.

38   Hall   Eng.

39   Parlor   Hall   Va.

40   Hall   Parlor   Eng.

41   Hall   Parlor   Va.

42   Hall   Tapestry R.   Eng.

43   Great Hall   East Room   H.C.F.   Va

44   Great Hall   Eng.

Virginia are several examples which form a definite school of building, characterized as follows.

As we know it, the Virginia hall-and-parlor house was brick, about twenty feet by forty in size, with chimneys at the gables. Some of the chimneys projected from the gable wall and were termed "pyramid" chimneys because of their shape. The stacks were tall and T-shaped in plan. There were steep roofs, some of which inclined as much as 54 degrees from the horizontal. There were no dormers to light the loft — only small lie-on-your-stomach windows [8] in the gables. The first-story windows and doorways were arched, and the main doorway was off the center of the dwelling. Sometimes the simple boxed cornices were stopped by brick corbels, or brackets, other times by curved end-boards. The brickwork was laid in either the Flemish or the English bond.[9] Such was the type of yeoman's habitation seen along the James and York Rivers by travelers newly arrived in the Colony.

The foremost example of the hall-and-parlor cottage is the brick Adam Thoroughgood House in Princess Anne County, Virginia, dating possibly from 1640, or soon afterward (Figs. 47, 54). In the matter of the date of erection it is well to be sceptical about the "illegible" brick reported to have been read at Thoroughgood's twenty or thirty years ago.[10] Originally all the windows were leaded casements, those on the long sides of the dwelling having mullions and transoms. There are the customary lie-on-your-stomach windows in the attic. Noteworthy are the chimneys, which are T-shaped, following the medieval method of breaking up the stacks into "projections and settings forward," because of the love of novelty and change. The south chimney, a projecting "pyramid," has long, steep weatherings or slopes, which are tiled. Along the rake, or sloping edge, of the gables are lines of glazed header bricks — a medieval feature which is so ancient that it harks back beyond England to Normandy of the eleventh century.

Another hall-and-parlor abode is the brick Wishart House (Figs. 39, 45) in Norfolk, Virginia, said to have been erected about 1680. Shorter than Thoroughgood's, it nevertheless retains the same width. The doorways have segmental arches of glazed brick, but the windows possess flat arches of rubbed or gauged brick.[11] In other words, this dwelling was built at a time when the use of the flat arch was just coming into style. The cornice, however, retains the medieval brick corbels at either end. Inside

---

[8] So named because they were set near the attic floor.

[9] See note 4, page 29. In Flemish bond the headers and stretchers alternate in each row or course.

[10] Waterman and Barrows (1932), pp. 3, 6.

[11] A kind of brick, introduced about 1630 in England, which has been rubbed smooth with a sharp sandstone to a uniform size.

the cottage, the staircase is boxed or partitioned with vertical, random-width boards — the medieval parclose or screened partition.

Sweet Hall (Fig. 50), of the Claibornes, in King William County, dating from about 1695, would fall into the hall-and-parlor classification, except for its rear wing. The tall chimneys, T-shaped (Figs. 75, 76), with weatherings half way up the stacks and elaborately designed caps, give this ancient pile an air of distinction. The little, arched, lie-on-your-stomach windows are reminiscent of those in the oldest structures of southwest Surrey, and lend a quaint flavor to the gable ends.

At Jamestown the demolished Sherwood mansion, erected between 1677 and 1680 on the site of the Governor's House (Fig. 48), departed slightly from the general run of hall-and-parlor houses in having the hall the same size as the parlor.[12] In its day, Sherwood's was considered a handsome residence and was noted in 1685 as the place where the government of Virginia met. In the "Great Hall," where His Majesty's Governor and Council sat, there was a large plaster coat-of-arms, and other ornamental plaster-work on ceiling or mantel. The arms were British and royal, and they carried the well-known motto of the Garter, thus: *Honi soit qui mal y pense.*

Such plaster decorations in England were known as pargetry or pargeting and embellished both the exterior and the interior of certain late sixteenth- and seventeenth-century dwellings.[13] At New Hall, Elland, England, there is a large plaster cast of the Royal Arms, dated 1670, situated above the fireplace. Still another is located on the ceiling of a room in the Star Chamber, Great Yarmouth.[14]

The next logical step in the development of the rural seat in Virginia was to partition off the hall in order to create a central passageway, forming the typical dwelling described in the next chapter. Nevertheless, there seems to have been in early Virginia what the English knew in the sixteenth century as the "double-parlor" house (Figs. 58, 60), where the hall stood between two parlors. The only example, as far as is known, was the Green Spring (Figs. 57, 59), built in or about 1646, in James City County, by the "iron Governor," Sir William Berkeley.

While not the first great house of the American Colonies, the Green Spring was nonetheless the show place of early Virginia. Although ninety-seven and a half feet long, the mansion kept to the customary medieval narrowness, being only twenty-four and a half wide. There were three rooms downstairs, and the same number on the second floor. An ell was later added at the rear.

Since the foundation walls are thick — twenty-eight inches — it is evident that the

[12] See Forman (1938), pp. 116ff.

[13] *Essex*, III, 235; Braun (1940), p. 75.

[14] Oliver (1912), pl. 31.

MEDIEVAL BRICK HOUSES OF VIRGINIA AND ENGLAND

45. Wishart House, Norfolk, Virginia, c. 1680. South gable and west side. (Reconstruction drawing by author after data from HABS)

46. House at Frodingham, near Scunthorpe, Lincolnshire, England. (After Oliver, 1929)

47. Adam Thoroughgood House, Princess Anne County, Virginia, c. 1640. (After Waterman and Barrows, 1932)

48. The Governor's House, Jamestown, Virginia, possibly as early as 1620. (After Ambler MSS, and Forman, 1938)

49. Kis Kis Kiack, York County, Virginia, c. 1700 (?). (After Worthington, 1918, and HABS)

50. Sweet Hall, King William County, Virginia, c. 1695.

51. House at South Cove, near Southwold, England. (After Oliver, 1929)

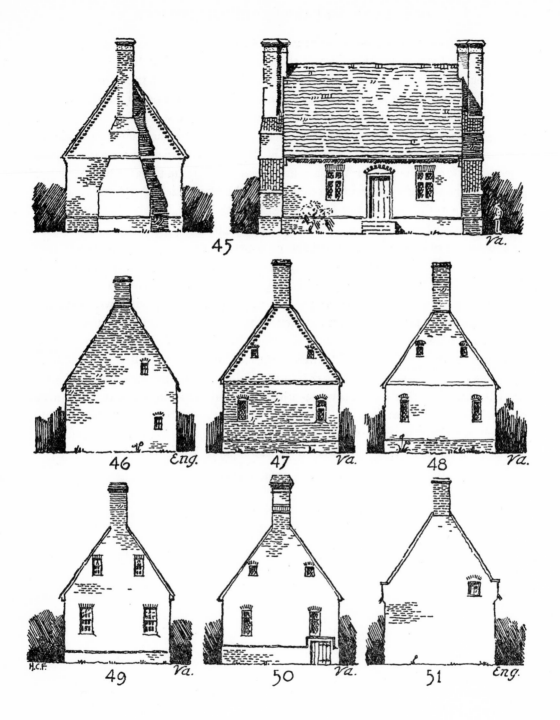

45

Va.

46 *Eng.*

47 *Va.*

48 *Va.*

49 *Va.*

50 *Va.*

51 *Eng.*

Green Spring was two full stories in height. On the front of the mansion, according to Benjamin H. Latrobe's pocket diary,[15] there was a porch having "some clumsy ornamental brickwork about the style of James the first"; that is, of the Jacobean design of the first quarter of the seventeenth century, which superimposed curved Flemish gables and classical Renaissance trimmings upon late Gothic structures. It is not surprising to find that the great Sir William Berkeley in 1646 or thereabouts was slightly ahead of most of his Virginia compatriots in the matter of keeping up with the new London classical fashions. Sir William had a way of being up-to-date; before his Virginia sojourns he had even written a play, called the "Lost Lady." Pepys saw it acted in London in 1661, and was not greatly pleased with it.

The reconstruction drawing of the Green Spring (Fig. 57) is based fundamentally on a measured plan of the foundation and on Latrobe's drawing of the proposed alterations of 1796. The design and planning of the porch are conjectural. From the foundation came the first piece of leaded diamond glass, or quarrel, discovered in Virginia; therefore, it is evident that the edifice carried lattice casement windows. When he called the Green Spring the "oldest inhabited house in North America," the architect Latrobe was ignorant of the thousands of earlier English, Spanish, French, and Dutch dwellings on this continent. With more truth he might have called it the longest and most individual mansion of its day in the Colony. The historian Bruce puts forward the stricture that in the seventeenth century no house in Virginia could make pretentions to beauty of design. Latrobe called the Green Spring a "brick building of great solidity, but no attempt at grandeur." Even so, Sir William, rich and fashionable, could scarcely have erected a mean-looking house.

[15] Quoted in Waterman and Barrows (1932). This was Latrobe, the American architect (d. 1820).

52. PINEWOODS OR WARBURTON HOUSE IN JAMES CITY COUNTY, VIRGINIA

An example of the central-passage type. Note the T-shaped chimneys.

53. THE TRIPLE "DIAMOND" STACKS OF BACON'S
CASTLE

While the chimneys are medieval, the fantastic curvilinear gables are
Jacobean. In Surry County, Virginia.

VI

THE TYPICAL COUNTRY HOUSE IN VIRGINIA

WHEN the hall, larger of the two rooms in the hall-and-parlor dwelling, was screened from the entrance by a partition, a passageway was thereby created, and the typical home, the central-passage type, was originated.

Yet, on the exterior, it is difficult to note the difference between a hall-and-parlor dwelling and one of central-passage type. Pinewoods, the Warburton House (Figs. 52, 55), for instance, built about 1680 in James City County, has the T-shaped chimneys, the steep roof (50°), the arched windows and doorways, similar to those of the Thoroughgood House already described. One exterior detail is different: the chimney stacks at Pinewoods have caps adorned with mouse-tooth brickwork — the bricks being placed on the diagonal to project like teeth — and have sloping brick setbacks from the face of the gables. The interior has unfortunately been burnt out, but originally there was a central passageway flanked by a room on either side. Each fireplace had a pair of closets.

Another example which probably dates from the very end of the seventeenth century is Kis Kis Kiack, a little brick abode (Fig. 49) in York County, which was named, not for kissing, but for an Indian locality. The fire which destroyed the entire interior did not demolish the outer shell. The slope of the gables indicates that the original roof had a pitch of 55°, one of the steepest in all Virginia. When Kis Kis Kiack was erected, arched windows and doorways had gone out of fashion, and the flat arch for wall openings was current. On the other hand, the chimneys retained the traditional T-shaped plan.

Both Pinewoods and Kis Kis Kiack have a façade design of central door flanked by windows, one on either side. When the Englishman wished larger rooms, he invented the "advanced" central-passage type, marked by *two* windows on either side of the main door. Such a dwelling is the brick Keeling House (Fig. 56), built about 1700 in Princess Anne County. It is seven feet longer, and one foot wider, than Pinewoods. The doorway, exactly in the center of the dwelling, has a transom light to illumine the narrow central passage within. Furthermore, the main windows have flat arches and sliding sash. There were probably no casements in the Keeling House, because

MORE MEDIEVAL TYPES OF VIRGINIA DWELLINGS

54. Adam Thoroughgood House, Princess Anne County, Virginia, c. 1640. South and east elevations. An example of hall-and-parlor dwelling. (After HABS, and Waterman and Barrows, 1932)

55. Pinewoods, or Warburton House, James City County, Virginia, c. 1680. South and west sides. Example of central-passage type. (After Kimball, 1935, and author's notes)

56. Keeling House, Princess Anne County, Virginia, c. 1700. East and north sides. Example of central-passage type. (After HABS)

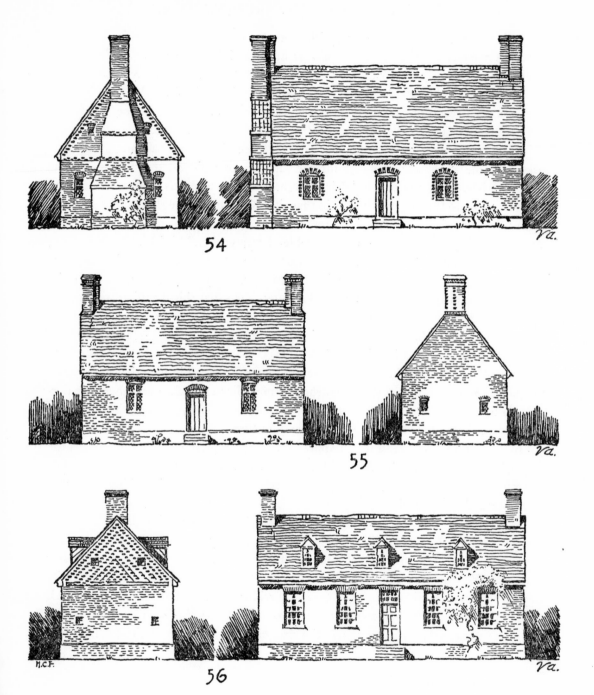

54

55

56

the sash represents an early shape which seems to have come into fashion about the time this habitation was built: the upper sash, three lights tall; the lower, two. The gables are distinguished by black glazing patterns, which, for lack of any known appropriate name, may be called "chevrons," that is, a series of inverted V's. To be sure, such glazed decoration was only one step further from the single line of glazing paralleling the rake of the roof, as on the Thoroughgood House.

In Jamestown there once stood a late seventeenth-century "advanced" central-passage home (Fig. 41), labelled for the sake of convenience, the "House on the Lands of Mr. John Watson and Mr. Knight." The house was situated parallel to and very close to the old Back Street in that city. Curiously enough, the dwelling was almost the same size as the Keeling House, had the same kind of flat arches of rubbed or gauged brick and had the same water table of "squynchon"[1] bricks.

Across the James from Jamestown stands another "advanced" central-passage example: old Smith's Fort Plantation, built in Surry County on land owned in 1614 by John Rolfe, husband of Pocahontas. All accounts state that this dwelling was erected in 1652 by their son, Thomas Rolfe,[2] but the architectural evidence, such as the segmental arches of beautifully rubbed brickwork over the doorways — a sophisticated motif probably not used in Virginia before 1700 — indicates a much later date than now accepted. Further, the chimneys are no longer T-shaped in plan, but plainly rectangular; the roof is not so steeply pitched as in earlier examples; and there are dormers to light the second floor. Smith's Fort Plantation marks, perhaps, the beginning of the transition to the Georgian period in architecture.

In England a homestead which approximates the typical Virginia dwelling is the original part of Latchley's Manor House (Fig. 42), at Steeple Bumpstead, Essex. Since it was erected at the beginning of the sixteenth century, it has chimneys at the side instead of at the gables.

The origin of the central-passage house in England was probably due to the same reasons as those of Virginia. The desire for more privacy in the great hall led to the erection of a screen or parclose at one end of the room. For example, in the lesser homes of Westmorland the peasants' and yeomen's cottages had the hall entered by way of a passage called a "hallen." Such a corridor was merely a section of the hall screened off by a partition known in those parts as the "heck." The front door opened into the passageway.[3] Undoubtedly, the original idea came from the twelfth- and

---

[1] Chamfered bricks, characteristic of thirteenth- and fourteenth-century England. Lloyd (1928), pp. 4ff.

[2] *VMHB*, XLII, 200.

[3] *Westmorland*, p. lxi.

thirteenth-century custom of placing a screened passage, or "screens bay," at the end of the lord's hall opposite the dais or raised platform. A case in point is the Manor Farm at Little Chesterfield, Essex, dating from 1200, where the screened passageway separated the great hall from the kitchen.

MEDIEVAL DOUBLE-PARLOR HOUSES AND A VIRGINIA PLOT PLAN

57. The Green Spring, James City County, Virginia, c. 1646. Probable example of double-parlor house. Shape of porch is conjectural. (Reconstruction)

58. Double-parlor dwelling near Mellis, Suffolk, England, seventeenth century. (After Braun, 1940)

59. The Green Spring, James City County, Virginia, c. 1646. First floor plan. (Reconstruction by author after cellar plan in Waterman and Barrows, 1932.) Compare with Waterman, 1946, p. 21.

60. Double-parlor dwelling, typical of seventeenth-century England. Block plan. (After Braun, 1940)

61. Bacon's Castle, Surry County, Virginia, c. 1650. Plot plan showing arrangement of dependencies. (After HABS)

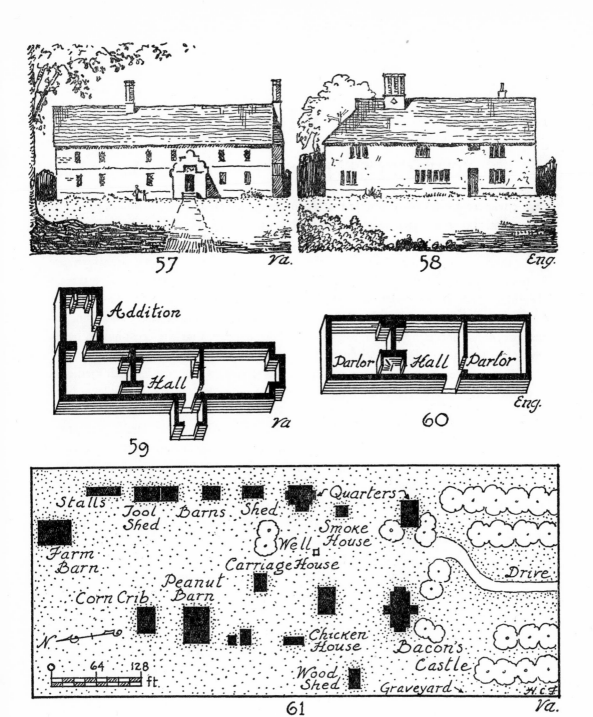

57   *Va.*

58   *Eng.*

Addition

Hall

59   *Va*

Parlor   Hall   Parlor

60   *Eng.*

Stalls   Tool Shed   Barns   Shed   Quarters

Farm Barn

Smoke House

Well

Carriage House

Corn Crib

Peanut Barn

Chicken House

Bacon's Castle

Drive

N.

64   128 ft.

Wood Shed

Graveyard

61   *Va.*

VII

THE CROSS-HOUSE IN VIRGINIA

I<small>T WAS</small> a comparatively simple matter to change a hall-and-parlor house, or one of central-passage type, to a cruciform structure. An enclosed entrance porch was placed on the front and a stair tower, or other kind of wing, at the rear — and there it was, the culmination of the development of the Virginia country house in the seventeenth century. Even so, it is not necessarily true that the more typical dwellings were all erected first, and all cross-edifices later. But indications are that known examples of the cruciform class average together a much later date than, for instance, the Thoroughgood House. It therefore appears that the cross-house, by its very complex nature, did not originate first, as has been recently suggested.[1]

The entrance porch or vestibule, and the stair tower, were pure English medieval features, and it is a pity that at least three out of seven known structures have been badly mutilated in the process of time, and that two have been completely razed from their foundations. Even in Maryland, the "most interesting of the larger plantation houses," [2] cruciform Bond Castle, was pulled down to make room for an ugly farm structure.

In England the cross-dwelling must have been derived from the parish church, and may have carried a religious connotation. To declare that it had such a meaning in Virginia and Maryland would be a stretch of fancy; but who can tell what was in the mind of the Southern planter when designing a house on a cross? The colonists of the seventeenth century were, by and large, a deeply religious people.

We know cruciform architecture in Virginia best through these seven sites: Bacon's Castle in Surry County; ruined Malvern Hill in Henrico County; the demolished Third State House at Jamestown, as well as the destroyed Fourth State House on the same site; the razed Turkey Island dwelling (Fig. 97), home of the well-known Randolph family in Henrico County; Foster's Castle and Christ's Cross in New Kent County; and lastly, the partially ravaged, original Matthew Jones House in Warwick County.

[1] Wertenbaker (1942), pp. 76–82.
[2] *Ibid*, p. 86.

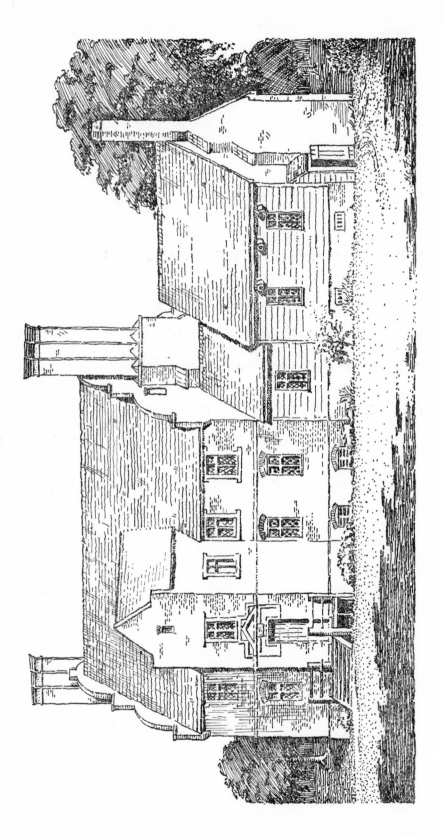

62. BACON'S CASTLE, SURRY COUNTY, VIRGINIA, C. 1650
(Reconstruction)

JACOBEAN GABLES IN VIRGINIA AND ENGLAND

63. Bacon's Castle, Surry County, Virginia, c. 1650. (After HABS)

64. Gable at Wingham, Kent, England. (After Dawber, 1900)

65. Gable at Whitehall, Hemingford Abbots, England, seventeenth century. (After *Huntingdonshire*)

66. Woodham Walter Church, Essex, England, 1564. (After *Essex*, II)

67. The Old Brick Church, or St. Luke's, Isle of Wight County, Virginia, c. 1682 (?). (After HABS)

68. Liscombe Park Chapel, Soulbury, England, c. 1350. (After *Buckinghamshire*, II)

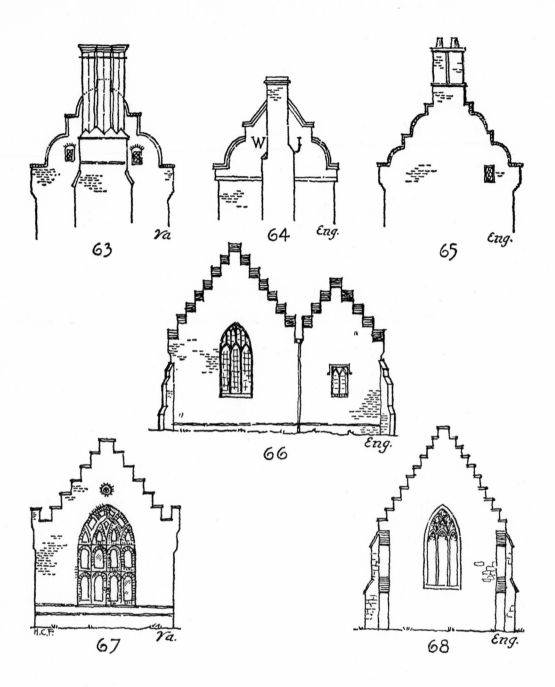

63 *Va*

64 *Eng.*

65 *Eng.*

66 *Eng.*

67 *Va.*

H.C.F.

68 *Eng.*

Sometimes the building was merely an incipient cross, with the back wing omitted altogether. John Holmwood's frame domicile, built about 1649 on Berkeley Plantation on James River, had a wooden six-by-ten-foot porch on the front, but there was only a shed all along the back side.

The names of the rooms are informative. The bedroom or office over the front porch was called the "porch chamber." Edward Lockey's home in Henrico County, we are told, had a hall, middle room, kitchen, chamber over the hall, small room at the rear of the chamber, an (attic) room over the chamber and a porch chamber.[3] William Fauntleroy appears to have had another house of this kind, on the Rappahannock River, comprising porch chamber, hall, closet, hall chamber, second chamber overhead, and kitchen. In Accomac, Southey Littleton had another dwelling with porch and porch chamber.

The most interesting of the cross-houses in Virginia, and the most important as well, is Bacon's Castle, or Allen's Brick House (Figs. 62, 96), believed to have been erected in 1655 by Arthur Allen, who in 1649 had arrived from England. When Nathaniel Bacon, leader of the Rebellion of 1676, sent his soldiers to seize the great dwelling, it must have been already standing for several years. It was named "Castle" in the sense of fort and is distinctive in Virginia because of its Jacobean gables (Fig. 63) of steps and cuspings. Bacon's is a medieval "castle" with Jacobean trimmings.

The curious curvilinear gables were derived about 1600, by way of England, from Flemish or Low Country Gothic gables. Thus they are known either as Jacobean or as "Flemish-by-way-of-England" gables. At the Skipper's House (1531) in Ghent, Belgium, the gables have the extravagant and fantastic curves which the Low Countrymen loved so well. About the time of James I the English began to refine and simplify the Flemish gable, in order to harmonize it with their own English medieval tradition.[4] Accordingly, we have British examples of the seventeenth century in Whitehall, Hemingford Abbots, Huntingdonshire; Stibbington Hall (1625), in the same shire; and Saling Hall (1699) in Essex.[5] These are three out of thousands. In this volume some English gables are illustrated (Figs. 64, 65) as a basis for comparison with those of Bacon's Castle in Virginia. The sweeping curves spring from corbeled parapets at the eaves — parapets which are themselves pure medieval features. On the crowns of the gables of Bacon's Castle there are small rectangular projections, resembling finials, which are almost concealed behind the chimney stacks.

Also designed in the manner of the Middle Ages are these same chimney stacks,

[3] Bruce (1896), II, 153.
[4] Gotch (1901), pp. 8, 120; Fletcher (1924), pp. 474, 475.
[5] *Huntingdonshire*, pl. 148; Messent (1928), pl. 128; *Essex*, I, 133.

triple in number at each gable of Bacon's Castle (Fig. 53), and set diagonally upon their massive bases. In the early sixteenth century, English chimney shafts were usually heavily molded, but in the latter part of this period they became plainer, were set square, or diamond-like (Fig. 70), and rose singly or in groups. In Yorkshire at this time the chimneys were almost invariably detached square shafts, one to each flue, and set diagonally. As at Bacon's Castle, such stacks almost always possessed plinths or washes,[6] engaged [7] molded caps, and strings or necking bands.

It is an interesting fact that another example of diamond stacks exists in Virginia. Winona, a little brick story-and-loft dwelling in Northampton County on the Eastern Shore, has three of these shafts on one chimney (Fig. 69). They rise separately from a solid, square base, and are engaged or joined at the caps. There are no plaster bands about the necking, however, as at Bacon's Castle; but on the caps and below the wash there are rows of mouse-tooth bricks, in the manner of those of Pinewoods, the War- burton House (1680), already described. The date of Winona has been suggested as 1645;[8] on the other hand, the "teeth" and the house-depth of two rooms indicates a date of about 1700 or later. In the early days, Virginia must have abounded with diamond stacks. Before it was destroyed about 1900, old Fairfield in Gloucester County had seven.

In truth, so interesting were the chimneys of Fairfield, or Carter's Creek Planta- tion, as it was sometimes called, that it might be well to digress for a moment upon this subject. The original brick structure was a two-story hall-and-parlor house (Fig. 89), believed to have been erected about 1692 by Lewis Burwell. The interior is sup- posed to have been noted for the Gothic linen-fold paneling. The windows had leaded casements and flat arches; the front door, uniquely placed at one side of the façade, held transom lights.

But it was the single end-chimney which formed the distinctive feature of the place. It comprised two diamond stacks set on a low base, which scarcely cleared the roof — an arrangement which had no known counterpart in this country, but which was common enough in England (Figs. 71, 72). Both caps and base were ornamented with mouse-tooth brickwork.

Probably soon after 1692, a wing was added to the north gable of Fairfield, and the twin stacks were duplicated. Surmounting the steep roof of the addition was a curious, squat dormer window, with two small casements. Still a second addition with diamond stacks was made in the early eighteenth century, a work which forms the subject of a later chapter.

[6] Sloping surface to cast off water; weathering.
[7] Joined at the top.

[8] Upshur and Whitelaw (1938).

GOTHIC CHIMNEYS IN VIRGINIA AND ENGLAND

69. Winona, Northampton County, Virginia. Diamond stacks. (After Forman, 1938)

70. House in Suffolk, England, late sixteenth century, showing typical diamond stacks. (After Hunter, 1930)

71. Fairfield, Gloucester County, Virginia, 1692. Diamond stacks from original portion of dwelling. (After photographs in Waterman and Barrows, 1932)

72. House in Gloucestershire, England, showing diamond stacks. (After Broadbent and Minoprio, 1931)

73. Matthew Jones House, Warwick County, Virginia, c. 1700 or before, showing square stacks. (After HABS)

74. Manor House, Lyddington, England, fifteenth century, showing square stacks. (After Garner and Stratton, II)

75. Sweet Hall, King William County, Virginia, c. 1695, showing T-shaped stack.

76. The White Hart Inn, Whitley, Surrey, England, showing T-shaped stack. (After Davie, 1908)

Virginia   69

England   70

Va.   71

Eng.   72

Va.   73

Eng.   74

Va.   75

Eng.   76

H.C.F.

77. Bacon's Castle, Surry County, Virginia, c. 1650. Approximate detail of pediment on main entrance.

78. Ripley Manor House, now Holes Cottage, Surrey, England. Main entrance detail. (After Davie, 1908)

79. The Old Brick Church, or St. Luke's, Isle of Wight County, Virginia, c. 1682 (?). Pediment on tower. Compare with Fig. 109. (After HABS)

80. House at Wroxham, Norfolk, England, c. 1610–1630. Pediments over windows. (After Oliver, 1912)

81. Make Peace, Somerset County, Maryland, c. 1663. Black diapering on east gable. Compare with Fig. 170. (After Forman, 1934)

82. Nether Hall, Roydon, Essex, England, late fifteenth century. Black diaper pattern in brick. (After *Essex*, 11)

83. Malvern Hill, Henrico County, Virginia, c. 1662. Diapering on east gable. Compare with Fig. 110.

84. Cradle House, Marksall, Essex, England, late sixteenth century. Diapering on chimney. (After *Essex*, III)

85. Fassit House, Worcester County, Maryland, early eighteenth century. Diapering on gable. (After Forman, 1934)

86. Long's Ferry, Rowan County, North Carolina, late eighteenth or early nineteenth century. Sometimes called the Alexander Long House, or Sowers Ferry. (After HABS)

Returning to our description of Bacon's Castle, we may note that years ago a woodcut of this cross-dwelling was published in *Frank Leslie's Illustrated Weekly*.[9] From the picture it is evident that the mansion had a frame kitchen and "curtain" [10] wing (Figs. 62, 101). The kitchen-curtain appendage was a common feature among Maryland and Virginia houses, and there were many examples in medieval England.

In the South the curtain, called a colonnade when columns were employed, was perhaps sociologically significant, because it kept at a distance from the master's family the slaves who cooked the meals. At the same time it behooves us to realize that as far back as the twelfth century in England there was a precedent for the curtain passageway, known as "penthouse" or "pentice," [11] consisting of a covered way between hall and kitchen, or a connecting alleyway or external stairway carrying a penthouse roof. At Winchester in England there was once a penthouse extending between the great hall and the kitchen for the use of the King's seneschals. In the thirteenth century His Majesty commanded the Sheriff of Wiltshire to construct a penthouse running from the Queen's Chamber to her wardrobe, to build a second one with a chimney at the head of his hall at Brill, and to mend a third, situated between the hall and chapel there. At St. Aylott's (c. 1500) in Saffron Walden, Essex,[12] are the remains of a penthouse (Fig. 101), of seventeenth-century date, stretching between the great hall and the outhouse, in exactly the Virginia manner.

According to the woodcut of Bacon's Castle, the vestibule doorway had at its head a molded brick, triangular pediment (Figs. 62, 77), of a kind which may be classified as incipient or embryonic. In other words, such a pediment is an early version of the classical detail beginning to appear in Jacobean England. Although the motif has been cut away and plastered over, there is enough remaining to show what it was like. Perhaps it was a counterpart of that at the Green Spring, which Latrobe described as having been adorned with clumsy Jacobean brickwork. In England in the early seventeenth century the embryonic pediment of Jacobean or Flemish stock was fairly common: examples may be noted at the Ripley Manor House, Surrey, and at a dwelling in Wroxham, Norfolkshire (Figs. 78, 80).

As has been indicated, the enclosed porch and stair tower, such as those of Bacon's Castle, were strong traits of English architecture of the Middle Ages. The porch seems to have originated in the Anglo-Saxon church. There is an example in the Church of St. Lawrence at Bradford-on-Avon,[13] built about 700 A.D., nearly a thou-

---

[9] Reproduced in Kimball (1927), p. 41; Waterman and Barrows (1932), p. 24.

[10] A low connecting passageway.

[11] Braun (1940), p. 21.

[12] *Essex*, I, 242.

[13] Fletcher (1924), p. 320.

sand years before Bacon's Castle. Among the later parish churches having entrance vestibules are those of Bradwell, Essex, of the twelfth century, and of Bishopstone, Herefordshire, of the fourteenth.[14] In the field of domestic architecture the vestibule was by the fourteenth century a frequent adornment of British homes, as exemplified by Lower Marston, Pencombe, Herefordshire, or Northborough Manor, Northamptonshire.[15] And in the sixteenth century it was widespread throughout England (Fig. 184).

The stair tower, too, has the same ancient ancestry. In the eleventh century Bishop Gundulf built for William the Conqueror the Tower of London with stair towers. When the English began to build manor houses, the feature became common. Three examples are Little Wenham of the thirteenth century; Latchley's Manor, Essex, of the seventeenth century; and Chantmarle Manor, Dorset, of the same period (Fig. 44). In this connection it is interesting to note that by 1600 the open-well stair with straight flights of steps around the sides of the tower was usually employed in place of the spiral stair. The staircase at Bacon's Castle was one of the open-well variety.

All the windows of Bacon's Castle originally possessed leaded casements with mullions and transoms. The first floor windows are arched in the medieval manner, but those on the second story at front and back have flat arches and Jacobean brick enframements (Fig. 62), which are borders of projecting bricks around the window openings, just as pictures are framed. The cellar was lighted by unglazed windows with horizontal square wooden bars, set diagonally in the frame. It is necessary only to compare a cellar window of Bacon's Castle with an English one, as at Benenden in Kent (Figs. 33, 34), to realize how much even in small details the provincial house was similar to the British.

After entering the enclosed vestibule at Bacon's Castle, one passes through a wide, arched doorway to the great hall (Fig. 96). On the left-hand side is the smaller chamber, the parlor, and directly ahead is a second arched door leading to the stair tower at the rear. Each of the two downstairs rooms has a ceiling which is divided into four parts by summer beams. So large are the fireplaces that the one in the cellar forms a small room in itself, eight feet long by three feet wide. The attic has a hooded fireplace (Fig. 11) reminiscent of medieval chimneys in England and France.

Not only did Virginians make use of the cross-house for country homes, but they employed it for public buildings. The destroyed Fourth State House (1685) at Jamestown, probably designed much like the Third, which it replaced, was a great

[14] *Essex*, III, 12; *Herefordshire*, III, 17.
[15] *Herefordshire*, III, 17; Tipping, p. 155.

TWO MEDIEVAL CROSS-HOUSES IN VIRGINIA

87. Foster's Castle, New Kent County, Virginia, 1685–1690. (Reconstruction drawing by the author, from HABS and Moorehead, 1934)

88. Christ's Cross, or Criss Cross, New Kent County, Virginia, c. 1690. (Reconstruction)

87

88

MEDIEVAL BATTLEMENTED DOORWAYS IN VIRGINIA AND ENGLAND

89. Fairfield, or Carter's Creek, Gloucester County, Virginia, about 1692. Reconstruction drawing of front elevation of original house. (After a photograph in Waterman and Barrows, 1932)

90. Christ's Cross, or Criss Cross, New Kent County, Virginia, c. 1690. Entrance doorway showing battlement.

91. Little Warley Hall, Essex, England, early sixteenth century. Entrance porch. (After *Essex*, IV)

89   Va.

90   Va.   91   Eng.

two-story cruciform structure (Fig. 23). In front there was a vestibule, and in the rear a stair tower, with a passageway connecting the two. On the left of the entrance was the large Court House Room, twenty-one feet by thirty-one, and on the opposite side, across the passageway, the Office of the Provincial Secretary. Upstairs, over the vestibule, was the "porch chamber," used as an office by the Clerk of the General Assembly. Likewise on the second floor were the Assembly Room, and the chamber where persons waited to do business with the Burgesses.[16]

The fireplaces of the Fourth State House were built as "side" chimneys, according to the sixteenth-century English fashion. Perhaps it was one of these very fireplaces which was responsible for the "unhappy accident" which resulted in the fire of 1698, when the Fourth State House went up in smoke. A year later James City was abandoned in favor of Williamsburg as the colonial capital.

Malvern Hill, third cruciform example (Figs. 43, 110), was built, it is believed, soon after 1662, and stands in ruins on the top of a high hill in Henrico County overlooking the James River. The writer was fortunate enough to make measured drawings of this brick house for the permanent records of the Library of Congress. The place was erected by Thomas Cocke, High Sheriff of the County, and figured in the notorious Battle of Malvern Hill in the Civil War. At the time of its destruction by fire in 1905, shells from hunting equipment kept on the second floor were passed through a window to prevent explosions, and wet quilts and blankets were spread out upon the steep roof. The entire dwelling was originally only one story and attic high, and the porch chamber was a diminutive sloped-ceiling nook above the arched vestibule. At the rear of the house stood, not a stair tower, but a twelve-foot-square parlor wing. According to a former occupant who lived at Malvern Hill for sixteen years, a staircase in the corner of the great hall rose to a landing about four feet above the floor, then turned and led to a dark upstairs passage and four bedrooms. Off the great hall was the "East Room," used as a dining room, and entered from a basement kitchen by a small winding staircase tucked away beside a towering chimney. The kitchen fireplace has two flues and is itself a little room, five and a half feet square.

The brickwork of Malvern Hill tells us a great deal about the masonry of the period. The large east and west end-chimneys were ornamented with lozenge or diamond patterns of glazed bricks (Fig. 83). Some of the lozenges were single; others were contiguous. The main windows had flat arches of salmon-colored rubbed brick, and the corners and round arches of the vestibule had the same kind of decoration. Curiously enough, the front of the enclosed porch had solid areas of brick glazing. In

---

[16] Forman (1938), pp. 167–173.

92. CHRIST'S CROSS, OR CRISS CROSS

A cruciform house in New Kent County, Virginia. The dotted lines illustrate original lines: compare Fig. 90.

93. THE TUDOR DOOR AT CHRIST'S CROSS, NEW KENT COUNTY,
VIRGINIA

The moldings are similar to those seen on Gothic chests.

the examination of the brickwork at Malvern Hill, the writer found that the huge end-chimneys originally belonged to a wooden house, possibly antedating 1662.

The diamond or lozenge pattern in brick is called "black diapering" in England. It is said that in the fifteenth century the motif was introduced into England from France,[17] but as a matter of fact there are designs of this sort upon an early fourteenth-century church at Ashington, Essex.[18] Not until the early sixteenth century do English buildings seem to have made universal use of the pattern, at which time such examples may be noted as the parish church of St. Andrew, Rockford, Essex; Nether Hall, Roydon, in the same shire (Figs. 82, 84); and the Cradle House at Marksall, in Essex, as well. The most distinguished building decorated with black diapering was Cardinal Wolsey's Hampton Court Palace.

The two most interesting cross-dwellings in Virginia, built in the late seventeenth century, are Foster's Castle, known as "The Castle," and Christ's Cross, called "Criss Cross" for short. Both stand in New Kent County and were erected about the same time: the former by Colonel Joseph Foster probably between 1685 and 1690, and the latter by George Poindexter about 1690.[19]

The interest in Foster's Castle lies chiefly for us in the exterior (Figs. 87, 95). Now much altered, the habitation was T-shaped in plan and comprised a story and loft with a two-story enclosed vestibule. The gables had the customary arched lie-on-your-stomach windows; but it was the front façade which was distinguished by unusual features. First, the main windows were each ample enough to contain three casements in a row, separated by mullions. Secondly, the gable over the porch had an *oeil de boeuf* window, sometimes known as an oculus or bull's eye. In 1872 it was claimed by the gentleman who owned the Castle that this circular window was used for shooting Indians. Be that as it may, the opening is almost unique in early Virginia. The third feature is the broken belt course of brick over the two-leaf door of the vestibule, forming what is known in England as a "battlemented" doorway, a description of which follows.

The belt or string course of projecting brick at the level of the second story at Foster's Castle ornaments not only the two main gable ends, but extends around the whole vestibule. Now when the belt approaches the front doorway, it makes a right-angle break upward and over the head of the door. The illustration indicates how this was done. Inasmuch as the battlemented doorway decorated the approach front of many a seventeenth-century dwelling — including Bacon's Castle and Fairfield — it is

[17] Lloyd (1928), pp. 4ff.
[18] *Essex*, IV, xxxii.
[19] Rev. Arthur Gray's letter dated January 9, 1937, HABS; Moorehead (1935).

not surprising to find that it is a pure English medieval motif. At historic Compton Wynyates in Warwickshire, for instance, the two-story porch has a "battlemented pointed arch." Another coeval example (Fig. 91) is at Little Warley Hall, Essex.

The other late seventeenth-century cruciform house, Christ's Cross, has not been as well preserved as its twin, Foster's Castle, but there is the same story-and-loft dwelling with high vestibule (Figs. 88, 92, 94). After entering the enclosed porch of Christ's Cross by a battlemented doorway (Fig. 90), one finds oneself facing a double door to the great hall, called the finest Tudor door in all Virginia (Fig. 93). To designate it as such is scarcely an exaggeration. The two leaves are hung by strap hinges, the heavy nails of which are cushioned on small leather washers. The narrow door panels, rising vertically, comprise molded battens secured to wide boards by means of clinched, wrought-iron nails. So wide are the boards of the door that only two vertical planks are needed for each leaf. But what is most remarkable are the Gothic moldings (Fig. 99 a, b) of the battens and the proportions of the panels. In design these moldings approach those seen on Gothic chests.

Upon entering the great hall of Christ's Cross, one's attention is drawn almost at once to the summer beam or girder (Fig. 99) which runs from one gable-end fireplace to the other. This beam, and those running along the top of the walls, called wall plates, are elaborately carved with molded edges, terminating in lamb's tongues.[20] For all that, the most curious feature of Christ's Cross is the capital of the square oak post near the middle of the dwelling. Upon this capital there is carved in raised relief a heart-shaped shield, enclosing scrolls, with a strange impost [21] molding above — the ensemble partaking of that flavor belonging to grotesque carvings of Romanesque and Gothic sculpture. Here at Christ's Cross is no Renaissance carving, but a bas-relief of genuine medieval style. In every rib and sinew Christ's Cross bespeaks the Middle Ages.

Last of the cross-houses herein described is the Matthew Jones dwelling at Fort Eustis, Warwick County, Virginia (Figs. 98, 100). According to a date in the brickwork, it was erected in 1727, but the two gable-end chimneys are older. It is possible that they date from 1700, or before, and that they belonged to a timber-framed structure, as was the probable case at Malvern Hill. It is because the original house possibly dated from the seventeenth century that the Jones House is described here and not in a later chapter.

The chimneys of the Jones House (Fig. 73) are distinguished by their twin stacks, set, not diamond-like, as those at Bacon's Castle, but square with the base. Their

---

[20] The termination of a molding on the edge of a beam.

[21] The molding at the top of the capital directly supporting the beam.

caps are joined. Such square stacks are characteristic of many English buildings of late medieval style, notably West End Farm, near Chiddingfold, Surrey,[22] or Sulgrave Manor of the Washingtons (Fig. 74). At the rear of the Jones House is a perfect example of an outshut, or lean-to.

In short, the cross type in Virginia has examples which are outstandingly medieval in design and construction. Sometimes there is a bit of Jacobean or Flemish Gothic detail thrown in to enliven the compositions; but this variety adds spice to the appearance of a type which represents the culmination of the Virginia rural dwelling.

[22] Ambler (1913), p. 8; Green (1908), pl. 12.

MEDIEVAL CROSS-PLANS IN VIRGINIA

94. Christ's Cross, or Criss Cross, New Kent County, Virginia, c. 1690. Floor plan. "a," grotesque capital on pilaster, drawn in Fig. 99; "b," Tudor door, in Fig. 93. (Adapted from Moorehead, 1935)

95. Foster's Castle, New Kent County, Virginia, 1685–1690. Floor plan. (HABS, and Moorehead, 1934)

96. Bacon's Castle, Surry County, Virginia, c. 1650. Floor plan. Kitchen approximated. (Reconstruction by author based on HABS.) Compare with Malvern Hill plan, Fig. 43.

97. Turkey Island, Henrico County, Virginia, seventeenth-century home of the Randolph family; destroyed about 1865. Approximate plan of foundation.

98. Matthew Jones House, Warwick County, Virginia, 1727. Chimneys are 1700, or before. (Adapted from HABS)

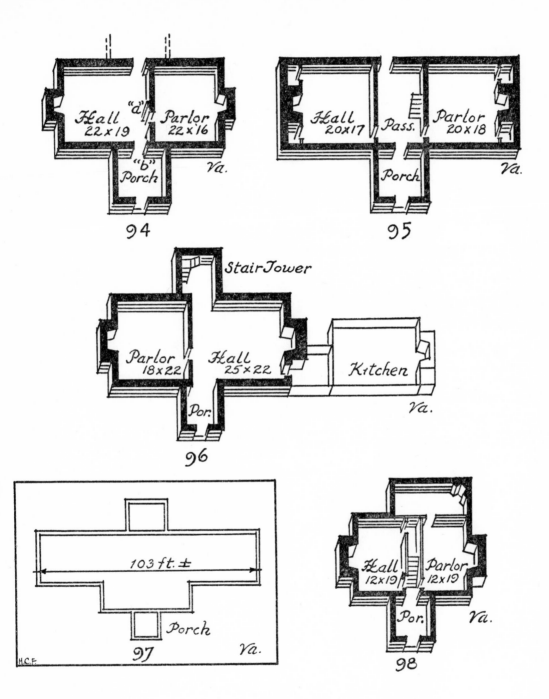

Hall 22×19 "a" Parlor 22×16

"b" Porch

Va.

94

Hall 20×17 Pass. Parlor 20×18

Porch

Va.

95

StairTower

Parlor 18×22 Hall 25×22 Kitchen

Por.

Va.

96

103 ft. ±

Porch

97 Va.

Hall 12×19 Parlor 12×19

Por. Va.

98

H.C.F.

CARVED WOODWORK, CHRIST'S CROSS, VIRGINIA

99. Christ's Cross, or Criss Cross, New Kent County, Virginia, c. 1690. The grotesque capital, and the summer beams with lamb's tongues.

99a. Christ's Cross. Gothic molding on the battens of the plank door.

99b. Magdalen College, Oxford, England, fifteenth century. Part of a Gothic molding from a doorway. (After Fletcher, 1924)

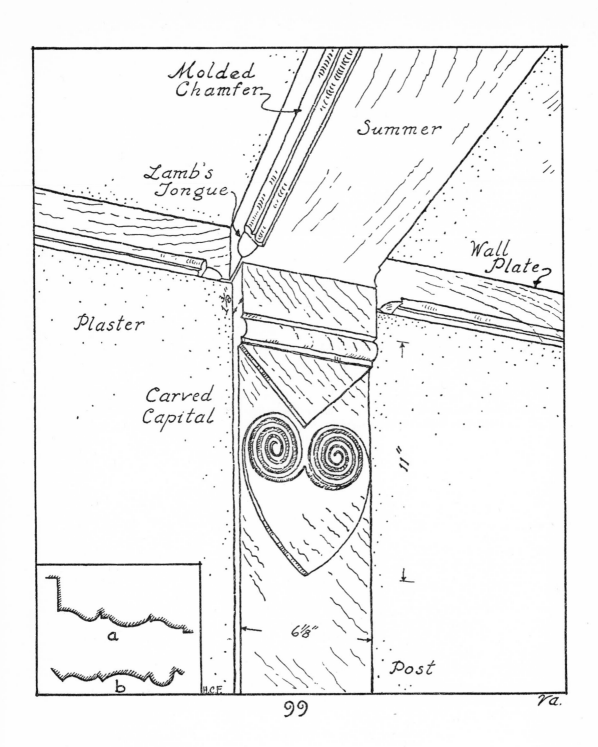

Molded
Chamfer

Summer

Lamb's
Tongue

Wall
Plate

Plaster

Carved
Capital

11"

6⅛"

a

b

H.C.F.

Post

99

Va.

ANOTHER VIRGINIA CROSS-HOUSE AND SOME MEDIEVAL CURTAINS

100. Matthew Jones House, Warwick County, Virginia, 1727. Chimneys are 1700, or before. (Reconstruction drawing by author from measured drawings of HABS)

101. Medieval curtains or penthouses in England and the Old South: block plans of, *left*, Preston, Calvert County, Maryland, 1652; *center*, St. Aylott's, Saffron Walden, Essex, England, c. 1500; *right*, Bacon's Castle, Surry County, Virginia, c. 1650.

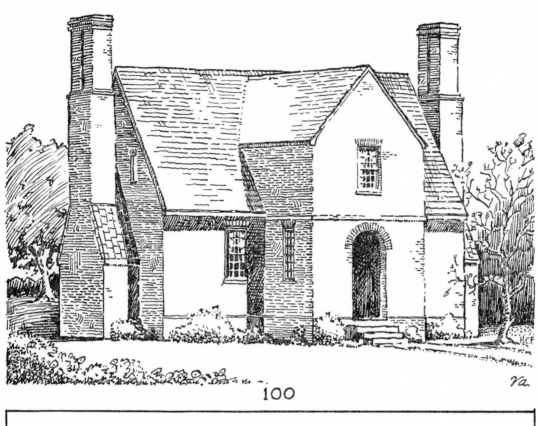

100   Va.

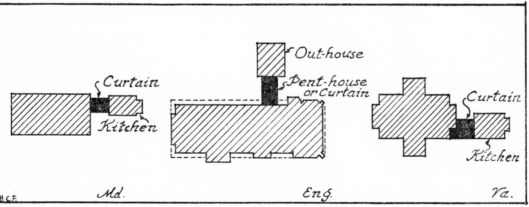

Curtain

Kitchen

Out-house

Pent-house
or Curtain

Curtain

Kitchen

Md.   Eng.   Va.

101

VIII

THE CROSSROADS CHURCH

IN seventeenth-century Virginia the churches were usually set down at the crossing of the highways, and their weather-beaten walls were dappled with shadows from tall pines. Such crossroads were nothing but footpaths or bridle trails meeting in the center of a cluster of plantations. Most of the churches were small and plain wooden fabrics, without bell towers.

As has been described, the first church in Virginia was a Gothic building, set on crucks or bent tree trunks. There were at least four other wooden chapels built on Jamestown Island before a substantial church of brick became an actuality. These frame houses of worship may be listed as follows for the sake of convenience:

1. The cruck church of 1607 (Fig. 4).
2. Lord Delaware's church of 1610, in size sixty feet by twenty-four, with two bells placed at the west end, and with casements which could be opened and shut according to the weather.
3. Argall's church of 1617, fifty feet by twenty. This may have been the "church in James City" which in 1623 had a "lattice gallerye" [1] for women and for visitors, and which in 1624 needed repairing.
4. A church, which was new in 1636, situated adjacent to the Reverend Thomas Hampton's land.

No traces of the first three edifices have been discovered at this writing. It seems that all authorities [2] declare that the third, or Argall's, church was built on the future site of the first brick church at Jamestown — that old structure of which only the ivy-clad tower remains today. This is, of course, an impossible hypothesis, since Argall's pile lay within the palisade, which was located one-half mile down James River from the Brick Church.[3] On the other hand, the present cobblestone and brick footings laid bare within the Brick Church represent possibly the fourth church, of 1636 vintage, placed near the Reverend Hampton's domain.

---

[1] Kingsbury (1933), IV, 138.
[2] Tyler (1906), p. 122; Yonge (1930), p. 67; Wertenbaker (1942), p. 87.
[3] See Forman (1938), chapter 11.

109. THE GOTHIC "OLD BRICK CHURCH," OR ST. LUKE'S, IN ISLE OF WIGHT COUNTY, VIRGINIA

Over the door is an embryonic pediment, like that at Bacon's Castle.

Except for the first, it is not possible to state exactly what kind or kinds of wooden construction were employed in these early sanctuaries. Perhaps many an early Virginia church was constructed of palisades of vertical planks stuck into the ground. In fact it is known that the first Lower Church, built probably in 1623, and located near Fishing Point on the Eastern Shore of Virginia, was "of insignificant dimension, constructed of roughly riled logs, cemented loosely with wattle." [4] As has already been pointed out, this is the Anglo-Saxon timber type of construction.

Among brick churches in this Colony there seem to have been two kinds: the aisleless nave type, with or without buttresses; and the cross or cruciform type, with apse.

No more definite proof of a religious architecture of the Middle Ages in Virginia is needed than three known examples of buttressed churches: the Old Brick Church, or St. Luke's, in Isle of Wight County; the ruined Jamestown Brick Church; and the demolished Second Bruton Church in Middle Plantation, now Williamsburg. So convincing an illustration of the medieval manner in religious architecture is the Old Brick Church in Isle of Wight (Fig. 109), built perhaps around 1632, but more likely about 1682,[5] that in the year 1907 it was taken as the model for the reconstructed Jamestown Brick Church (Fig. 102), originally completed in 1647. It was fortunate that both churches have similar brick towers and floor plans. Even the profiles of the brick window mullions were almost identical. Yet one delves into the realm of fancy when the proposal is made that the Jamestown Brick Church had the same "corbie" or "crow step" gables as those existing on the Old Brick Church in Isle of Wight County (Fig. 67). Of course it is possible that the two churches were designed by one builder, as has been advanced,[6] and therefore that the Jamestown example carried the curious Flemish gables of steps or "tabled offsets."

While the rugged tower of the Brick Church at Jamestown has been considerably mutilated, the belfry of the Old Brick Church stands pretty much as in days of yore. On the corners of the belfry are Jacobean brick quoins, and over the circular-headed doorway is an embryonic pediment (Fig. 79) of the kind that ornamented Bacon's Castle.

The Second Bruton Church, completed in 1683, was also of Gothic design, touched by Flemish influences (Fig. 104). There were shallow buttresses along its sides, but no tower. The gables were Jacobean, of curvilinear design, and had *oeil de boeuf* windows.

When the Virginians wished simpler structures, they omitted the buttresses, as, for

[4] Mason (1940).
[5] Mason (1943); Waterman and Johnston (1941) date the tower as "c. 1682."
[6] Wertenbaker (1942), p. 88.

MEDIEVAL CHURCHES IN VIRGINIA AND ENGLAND

102. The Brick Church, Jamestown, Virginia, completed after 1647. Front elevation and plan. (Reconstruction by writer after Forman, 1938)

103. Parish Church of St. Mary, Little Bentley, England, mid-fifteenth century. (After *Essex*, IV)

104. Second Bruton Parish Church, Williamsburg, Virginia, 1683, now destroyed. Floor plan and front elevation. (Reconstruction drawing by author after Michel's drawing of 1702, *VMHB*, XXIV, and foundation plan, Mason, April, 1939)

105. Parish Church of St. Margaret Bowers, Gifford, England, sixteenth century or earlier. Floor plan. (After *Essex*, IV)

106. Church at Moccas, England, twelfth century, showing apse. (After *Herefordshire*, I)

107. Pungoteague Church, known as the "Ace of Clubs," Accomac County, Virginia, c. 1666–1667. Compare with Fig. 106. (After Mason, Oct., 1941)

108. Yeocomico Church, Westmoreland County, Virginia, 1706, showing a Gothic tracery motif over entrance doorway.

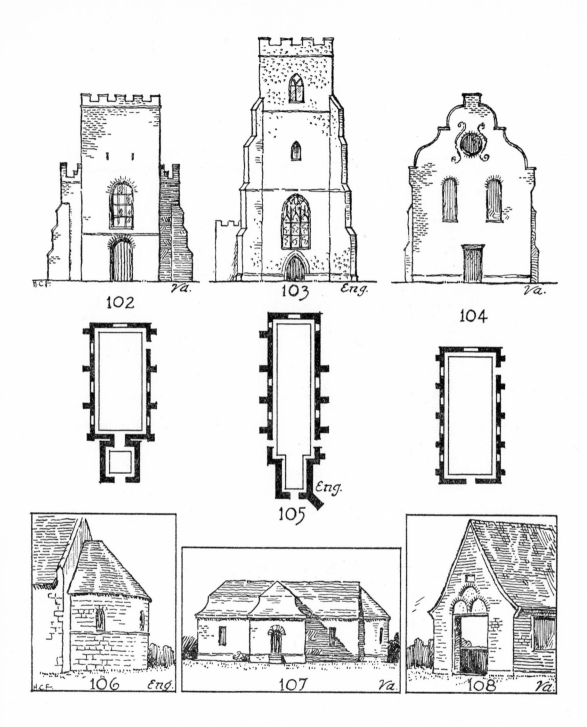

102   *Va.*

103   *Eng.*

104

105   *Eng.*

106   *Eng.*

107   *Va.*

108   *Va.*

110. MALVERN HILL, HENRICO COUNTY, VIRGINIA
A cruciform dwelling now in ruins. Note the porch and porch chamber.

instance, in the Merchant's Hope Church, Prince George County, dating perhaps from about 1657.

The aisleless nave church is common to England. Anglo-Saxon are the square chancel end and the tower at the entrance gable, which we may find incorporated in the Corbridge church, Northumberland.[7] In Essex, the church of Tollesbury, dating from the eleventh century, and that of St. Margaret Bowers, Gifford, of the sixteenth century (Figs. 103, 105), have floor plans much like their Virginia companions.

The Flemish crow step gable was freely employed in Kent and East Anglia during the sixteenth century. The Old Brick Church in Isle of Wight County, Virginia, has been aptly compared to Woodham Walter Church, Essex,[8] of 1564 vintage (Figs. 66, 67, 68). Other step gables exist in Buckinghamshire, Hertfordshire, and other counties. So loving was the Englishman toward crow steps that he placed them not only on gables, but also on chimneys and towers (Figs. 226, 243, 244).

The second class of brick church in Virginia of this period is cruciform, if the Pungoteague Church, known as old St. George's (Fig. 107), is as ancient as it is claimed to be. The date of its construction has been proposed as about 1656. Located in Accomac County, Virginia, it was in the shape of a Latin cross with an apse at the east end. Because of the form, the card-playing gentry called it the "Ace of Clubs" Church. The doors were round-arched, and the roof was a hipped gambrel or mansard. Undoubtedly the building was very quaint, and it is a pity that today it is only a ghost of its former self.

It is believed that the apse or rounded-end motif infiltrated into England from the Continent several centuries before the cruciform plan (Fig. 106). While there are a number of pre-Conquest cruciform churches in England, a cross with an apse is a rarity. The Saxon church at Worth, Sussex, appears to be, however, an example comparable to old Pungoteague.[9]

[7] Brown (1926–37), II, 296.
[8] Briggs (1932), p. 196; *Essex*, II, 271.
[9] Brown, II, fig. 171; Prior, pp. 52, 56; *Herefordshire*, III, 17.

IX

THE PERSISTENCE OF THE MEDIEVAL STYLE INTO THE NINETEENTH CENTURY

IT IS not generally known that the true medieval style — not the Gothic Revival — continued in Virginia all through the eighteenth century, and well into the nineteenth. Although the medieval period in architecture may be said to have ended about 1700, the tradition of the Middle Ages carried on, like a dying tidal wave, into the succeeding centuries.

At the commencement of the eighteenth century there were three styles of building in Virginia. The first was the medieval, perhaps influenced here and there with minor classical Georgian details, but otherwise unchanged. Then there was the transitional style, a stage of development between the Middle Ages and the Georgian. Lastly, the Georgian itself, which was first represented on a grand scale by the Governor's Palace in Williamsburg. This third style does not concern the subject of this volume.

The introduction of the sash window is a good barometer to indicate the change from the ancient to the modern style. This kind of window was not double-hung with weights and pulleys, as we know it. Instead, it was a crude sliding "guillotine" window, which had a tendency to fall suddenly on wrist or neck. The following table compares the first sash known in England with the first in Virginia:

England	*Virginia*
1519: Medieval leaded-glass wooden "leaves," sliding up and down.[1]	1699: Sash specified for the Capitol, Williamsburg.[3]
1630–6: Sash used at Raynham Park, Norfolk.[2]	1700: Sash ordered for a new brick church in St. Peter's Parish, New Kent County.
1672: Sash at Groombridge Place, Kent.	1700–10: Sash in existing Tabb House, York County.
1685: Modern sash with weights and pulleys used at Whitehall Palace, London.	1713: Sash used in Governor's Palace, Williamsburg. Etc., etc.

[1] Lloyd (1931), p. 70.   [2] Briggs (1932), p. 88.   [3] Hening, III, 420.

From this table it will be seen that it took all of fifty years and more, that is, from 1630 to 1699, for the sash window to "spread" to Virginia. At the same time the reader should be warned that all Virginia windows were not translated into sash in the first decade of the eighteenth century. In the same way that most Yorkshire houses retained the many-mullioned casement window until well into the eighteenth century,[4] so the dwellings and public buildings of Virginia were slow to change to new fenestral fashions. For example, in 1704, Major Nicholas Merriwether sent to England for glass, lead, solder, and casements for the "chapell" in St. Peter's Parish, New Kent County. In 1708, one Littlepage was ordered to erect on the glebe land of this same parish a dwelling-house, thirty-six feet by eighteen in size, with the customary medieval "Latches, Catches, Hinges, Locks, Glass and Casements." Even as late as 1733, a year which may be designated as "well into the eighteenth century," casement windows were specified for another glebe house in the same parish.[5] How true it is, that the coming of the new manner was gradual, the passing of the old was slow.

There penetrated into the eighteenth century the four chief types of dwellings described in the development of the medieval country house in Virginia. There is the one-bay cottage, represented by quaint Gunn's Run (Fig. 146), in Charles City County, before additions were made. There is the hall-and-parlor habitation, typified by Littlepage's Glebe house (Fig. 116), once standing in Charles City County.

When examples of the central-passage, or "typical," house are looked for, there are many eighteenth-century representatives from which to choose. Among timber-framed structures are Brick Billy, or Green Oak Farm (Fig. 117), of the Christian family, in New Kent County; Greenway, the birthplace of John Tyler, in Charles City County; the Custis House in Accomac; and the Montague House (Fig. 118) in Williamsburg. Then there is the brick Tabb House (Fig. 113) in York County, erected just after the turn of the eighteenth century. All these dwellings have plans of medieval type, but there can be seen in the design of some of the details a certain freedom, which foretells the new manner. For instance, the Custis House has at the foot of its winding staircase an archway with wooden pilasters of classical derivation. Again, the Tabb House has a closet underneath the stairs with a small window adjoining the back door — hardly a seventeenth-century arrangement.

In the eighteenth century the cruciform dwelling is well represented by the Matthew Jones House, the main brick walls of which date from 1727 (Figs. 98, 100). This habitation has been described in a previous chapter.

It is especially in the design of the gable that the persistence and continuity of the

---

[4] Ambler (1913), p. 8.
[5] *Vestry Book, St. Peter's*, p. 675.

THE PERSISTENCE OF THE MEDIEVAL STYLE IN EIGHTEENTH-CENTURY VIRGINIA

111. Huggins House, Princess Anne County, Virginia, early eighteenth century.

112. House at Great Tey, England, late sixteenth century. (After *Essex*, III)

113. Tabb House, York County, Virginia, just after 1700. (Kimball, 1935)

114. Eastwood, Princess Anne County, Virginia, eighteenth century. Compare with Fig. 165. (After HABS)

115. Skiff's Creek House, James City County, early eighteenth century.

116. Littlepage's Glebe House, New Kent County, Virginia, 1708. Block floor plan showing fireplaces with wood-and-plaster backs. (Conjectural reconstruction)

117. Brick Billy, or Green Oak Farm (original part), New Kent County, Virginia, eighteenth century. Example of the central-passage type.

118. Montague House, or Bracken House, Williamsburg, Virginia, eighteenth century. (After Kimball, 1935)

119. Gaines Farm Quarters, Hanover County, Virginia. Compare with Fig. 121. (After HABS)

120. Greenway Slave Kitchen, Charles City County, Virginia, eighteenth century. Note freestanding chimney.

121. Gaines Farm Quarters, Hanover County, Virginia, eighteenth century. Compare with Fig. 119. (After HABS)

122. Towles Point, Lancaster County, Virginia, c. 1711. Block plan showing transitional house with "cells" at rear. (After HABS)

123. Dahl's Swamp, or Topping House, Accomac County, Virginia, eighteenth century. Note single "cell."

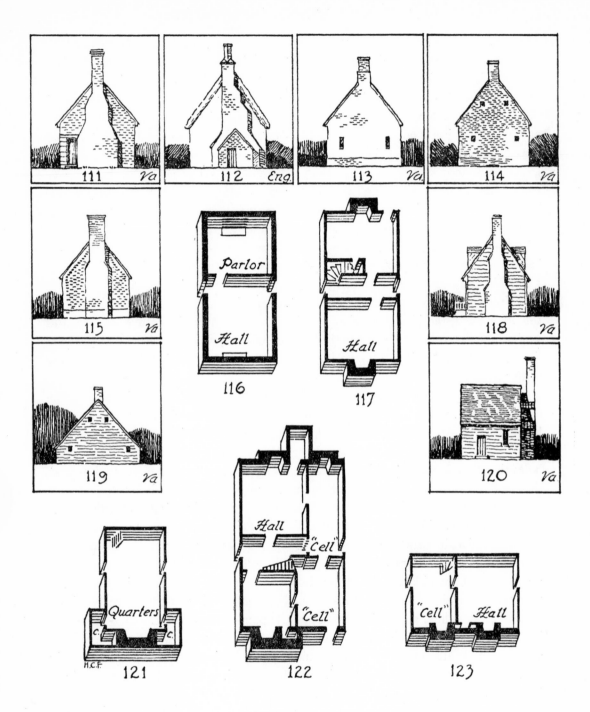

111 *Va* 112 *Eng.* 113 *Va* 114 *Va*

115 *Va*

116

Parlor

Hall

117

Hall

118 *Va*

119 *Va*

120 *Va*

121

Quarters

C. C.

H.C.F.

122

Hall

"*Cell*"

"*Cell*"

123

"*Cell*" *Hall*

medieval tradition is most visible. By and large, the gable-end compositions of the following examples are much the same as those of the preceding century: the Huggins House (Fig. 111) in Princess Anne County has the same kind of pyramid chimney as that on the medieval Thoroughgood House in the same county. Skiff's Creek House (Fig. 115) in James City County has the same glazed brick decoration along the rake of the roof as has Thoroughgood's. The Thomas Thornton dwelling in Accomac County possesses the same chevrons on the gable as does the earlier Keeling House, already described (Figs. 134, 56). In Northampton County the Fisher House even makes use of "black diapering" in a large way. Further, note the similarity of the Tabb House gable with that of seventeenth-century Warburton House, called Pine-woods (Figs. 113, 55). Finally, the gable of the destroyed Overseer's House [6] on King Carter's plantation, Corotoman, in Lancaster County, perhaps dating from 1700, had a roof line sloping 60° to the horizon — possibly the steepest in Virginia (Fig. 135). What a coasting the eighteenth-century children might have had!

Hitherto, the story-and-attic house, one room thick, has been considered here; on the other hand, the ideal Georgian mansion of the eighteenth century was two full stories high, as well as two rooms thick. Somewhere in between these two extremes lie the transitional buildings, savoring of both styles and yet holding more of the Gothic manner than the neoclassic.

The Georgian goal of larger rooms, higher ceilings, more open stairways, and an air of elegance, pleased the tobacco planter, who had become richer or whose family had increased. Accordingly, some of the little, narrow Virginia cottages were erected with a "cell" or "aisle" [7] at the rear. In truth, so slender were some of these cubby-holes that they looked more like aisles or passages than anything else. In England, they were the outshuts on the side of the house; in New England, lean-tos.

In this manner germinated the first kind of transitional dwelling, where the rooms are two chambers in depth. Although Towles Point, built about 1711 by Henry Towles, Junior, in Lancaster County, Virginia, possesses two back cells, the dwelling still keeps its story and loft, steep roof and ingle recesses (Figs. 122, 132, 145). Other mementoes of that ilk are the Richardson House (Figs. 124, 125) in James City County, where the passage extends along one gable end, and there are two ingle recesses at the other; and Dahl's Swamp, or Topping House (Figs. 123, 133), standing lonely as a scarecrow in an Accomac swamp. The latter is a dwelling where there is no passage at all, but only a little cell tucked away behind the great hall. When the roof has a longer slope at the rear than at the front, it is known as a "catslide," and

---

[6] Sometimes incorrectly called the Spinning House.
[7] Motif was probably derived from the church side aisle.

there are examples at the Binford House in Southampton County and Belmont in Lancaster County (Figs. 128–131).

One of the most medieval-looking cottages of this period is the Gaines Farm Quarters in Hanover County (Figs. 119, 121). This cabin — and it is little more than that — with its one large room and small ingles, or sleeping closets, projecting like warts on each side of the great fireplace, must have had its counterpart in the medieval English booth or stall. The east façade with its four tiny square windows and its eaves close to the ground is unique in Virginia. On the interior the post-and-lintel construction is exposed, as in the timber-framed cottages of the Middle Ages, and the ceiling was once probably open-timbered.

When the eighteenth-century planter did not thicken his home by adding cells at the rear, he enlarged the building vertically, while preserving the one-chamber thickness of medieval flavor. Two-storied Ringfield, built of brick about 1720–1725, in York County, was a noteworthy specimen of this second kind of transitional dwelling. The tall and slender gable ends of Ringfield, carrying imposing chimneys with sunken panels, must have impressed the beholder with their Gothic verticality. Another example is the frame Dr. Lucas House (Fig. 142) in New Kent County, where a seventeenth-century type of floor plan is preserved, even to the winding stairs in the central passage.

There were other methods of expanding the house. The third kind of transitional habitation is that with the gambrel roof, or roof of double slope on two sides only. The English appear to have instituted the gambrel roof in the Tudor period. One may view it in the great hall of Hampton Court Palace, dating from 1530–32, and in other buildings of southeast England. Ostensibly, it was one of the keys to the puzzle of how to gain more space in the attic. In Virginia one of the oldest gambrels is on the Reveal West House, erected about 1700 in Accomac County (Figs. 136, 137). This wooden cottage has a windowless brick gable, and a floor plan like that of the earlier Wishart House (Fig. 39), already described. The gambrel gives a "kick" at the eaves very much in the manner of the Dutch roof of New York. The winding staircase is partly boxed, and there is space enough upstairs under the spacious gambrel for three bedrooms.

Other gambrel-roofed dwellings in the eighteenth century are Salisbury Plain in Princess Anne County, Toddsbury in Gloucester County, and Watervale, now Windsor Shade (Fig. 139), in King William County. This last example is perhaps unique for its two-story brick chimney pent or ingle recess. Perhaps the most peculiar gambrel roof structure in Virginia was old Bewdley in Lancaster County, of about 1700.[8] Be-

---

[8] Earle (1929), p. 81; Waterman and Barrows (1932), p. 12.

MORE DWELLINGS OF MEDIEVAL STYLE IN
EIGHTEENTH-CENTURY VIRGINIA

124. Richardson House, James City County, Virginia, eighteenth century. A frame house with two projecting ingle recesses. (After HABS)

125. House at Dunley, Worcestershire, England. Compare with Fig. 124. (After Ingemann, 1938)

126. Point Pleasant, Surry County, Virginia, eighteenth century.

127. House near La Grange, Gloucester County, Virginia. (After HABS)

128. Binford House, Southampton County, Virginia, eighteenth century.

129. Cottage near Battle, England. Compare with Fig. 128. (After Hunter, 1930)

130. Barn near Yelding, Kent, England, showing "catslide" roof. (After Braun, 1940)

131. Rose Garden, New Kent County, Virginia. (After *WMQ*)

132. Towles Point, Lancaster County, Virginia, c. 1711. Compare with Fig. 146. A transitional house. (After HABS)

133. Dahl's Swamp, or Topping House, Accomac County, Virginia, late eighteenth century. Compare with Fig. 123.

134. Thomas Thornton House, Accomac County, Virginia, eighteenth century, showing black diapering.

135. Overseer's House at Corotoman, Lancaster County, Virginia, c. 1700 (?), now destroyed. Has a flush chimney with English bond. (After HABS)

136. Reveal West House, Accomac County, Virginia, early eighteenth century. A frame house with brick gables and a gambrel roof with "kicks." (After HABS)

137. A gambrel-roofed dwelling in Essex, England. (After *Essex*, IV)

138. Seven Springs, King William County, Virginia, eighteenth century. Note jerkin-headed roof. (After HABS)

139. Windsor Shade, formerly Waterville, King William County, Virginia, eighteenth century. Here the ingle recess is two stories.

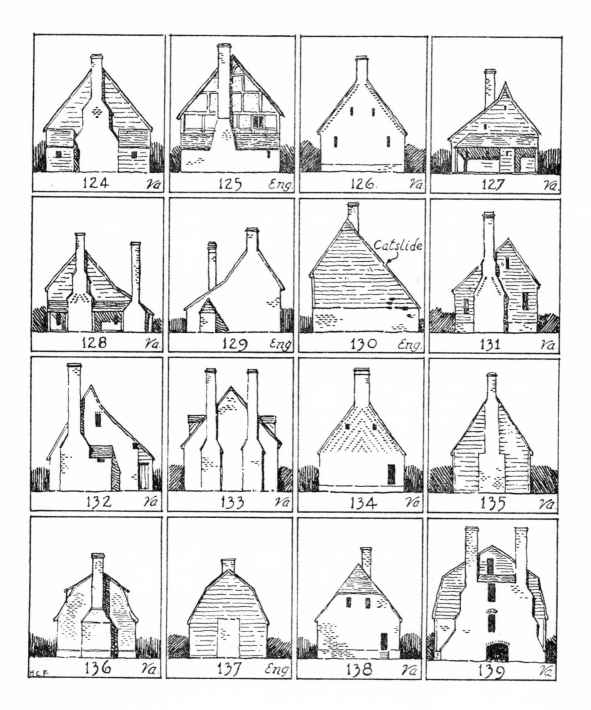

124   Va.

125   Eng.

126.   Va.

127   Va.

128   Va.

129   Eng

Catslide

130   Eng.

131   Va.

132   Va.

133   Va

134   Va

135   Va.

H.C.F. 136   Va.

137   Eng

138   Va.

139   Va.

THE PERSISTENCE OF MEDIEVAL STYLE IN EIGHTEENTH- AND NINETEENTH-CENTURY VIRGINIA

140. Fairfield, or Carter's Creek, Gloucester County, Virginia, showing the early eighteenth-century wing with diamond stacks. (After an old photograph in Kimball, 1927)

141. Grange Farm, Radwinter, Essex, England, sixteenth century. Compare these diamond stacks with those in Fig. 140. (After *Essex*, I)

142. Dr. Lucas House, New Kent County, Virginia, early eighteenth century. An example of transitional type. (After HABS and *WMQ*)

143. Merchant House, Dumfries, Virginia, early nineteenth century. Note Gothic verticality of chimney, and the inset arch. (After HABS)

144. Abingdon Glebe, Gloucester County, Virginia, c. 1700. Another transitional example, showing balanced end-pavilions. (After *WMQ*)

140

141 Eng.

142

143

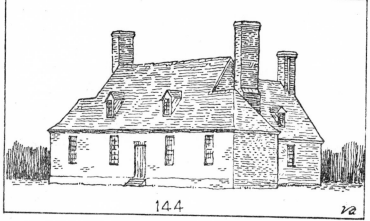

144

fore its destruction by fire in 1917, the mansion was two rooms deep with a roof "shingled" with dormers; in other words, there were two rows of dormer windows, one above the other.

The hip, or hipped, roof dwelling may be classified as the fourth chief type of transitional dwelling in Virginia. In the early days a hip was often called a "pyramid," and examples are found in England in the first half of the seventeenth century, as at Inigo Jones's Pendell, in Surrey, of 1636. And in Gloucestershire, for instance, hipped roofs are rarely found in the earliest homes, but they appear in the transitional examples of the late seventeenth and early eighteenth century.

The Georgian ideal was, of course, a mansion hipped on all sides, so that no "ugly" medieval gables could break up the level cornices.

A good specimen of the hip roof in Virginia was situated on the wing at Fairfield, Gloucester County.[9] This low story-and-loft appendage (Figs. 140, 141) was erected after 1700, and not in 1692 as the chimney brace indicated before the fire. It is more than probable that the chimney brace carried the date of the original house (Fig. 89), already described in an earlier chapter. Upon the hip roof of Fairfield stood three eighteenth-century diamond stacks, with engaged caps, and a group of four red tiles ornamenting the base of the chimney. The brick wall below the stacks had a series of holes in a row for doves, in other words, a dovecot. In medieval England, it may be remembered, only lords of the manor were permitted to keep doves.

An eminent example of transitional house with hipped roof is the Abingdon Glebe (Fig. 144), built of brick about 1700, in Gloucester County. In plan a "T," the dwelling represents an early example of the formal design in Virginia architecture. The long, low façade is exactly balanced, with hipped pavilions on either flank.

Another variety of the hip roof is the jerkin, a kind of miniature or incipient hip located up near the crest or ridge of the roof. In Virginia this is found on such eighteenth-century dwellings as brick Seven Springs (Fig. 138) in King William County, or wooden Bathurst in Essex County.

While four chief kinds of transitional housing have been stressed, it should not be forgotten that the medieval type, distinguished by the one-room-thick, story-and-attic cottage, with pointed gables, was predominant numerically in the first half of the eighteenth century. The Gothic died hard in Virginia. A walk down Duke of Gloucester Street in Williamsburg should convince any observer that little story-and-loft dwellings were numerous at this time. Even the twenty-by-forty and sixteen-by-twenty-four stock sizes of early Jamestown homes continued to be employed in this

---

[9] Not Fairfield, but the Court House of Talbot County, Maryland, 1680, seems to be the first authenticated hip-roofed house in the country. See Waterman (1946), p. 26.

eighteenth-century city. In this respect, it is not generally realized that the great Georgian mansions of Virginia were in many ways bound to medieval traditions. The medieval type of arched window heads are found in Westover (1726), Stratford (1725–30), Ampthill (c. 1732) and others. At Ampthill the brickwork is laid up in the English bond, a unique example in the eighteenth century. The main doorway of Stratford has a truncated brick pediment, similar to that of Bacon's Castle of a previous age. In addition, the whole appearance of the eighteenth-century dependency was medieval in flavor. Such outbuildings were nothing but the little narrow cottages hitherto described at some length (Fig. 120). The dependency chimney at Westover was originally much like the seventeenth-century "pyramid" chimney. An outbuilding at Carter's Grove (1751) is marked by lines of glazed header bricks paralleling the rake of the gable — a feature of many seventeenth-century homes.

And so the great formal edifices, towering above their elegant boxwood gardens and well-clipped driveways, could not escape the heritage of the previous hundred years, and before. At the ends of the garden lanes, or balancing the great house on either side, or hidden behind the cornfields, stood the little, thin, story-and-garret cottages, strongly savoring of the Middle Ages.

After the Revolutionary War the medieval style in Virginia architecture became weaker, but it did not discontinue. We have already noted in a previous chapter how Road View Kitchen carries a nineteenth-century wooden chimney. Other important examples erected in this century are the Merchant House in Dumfries, Prince William County, a tall, narrow edifice with T-shaped chimneys comprising stacks joined by arches (Fig. 143); Grove Hill in James City County, a wooden story-and-loft cottage of the 1830's; and Cedar Circle [10] in King William County.

The architectural style known as the Gothic Revival began in the early nineteenth century, and it is strange to find survivals of the true Gothic standing side by side, so to speak, with the pseudo-Gothic structures. It is stranger still to realize that in the 1830's, when the Gothic Revival commenced its popularity, nothing — not a whit — was known about the remnants of true Gothic upon our very doorstep. Then, the Old Brick Church, called St. Luke's, in Isle of Wight County, was all but unknown. Who cared to study Fairfield in Gloucester County before its destruction by fire? What a paradox to find that a century ago men endeavored to spread their own brand of birthday-cake Gothic throughout the country, when hundreds of real Gothic models stood nearby in the pine forests of the tidewater!

[10] *WMQ*, 2nd ser., v. 17, 528; v. 18, p. 530.

X

A SUMMARY OF THE VIRGINIA STYLE

DURING the seventeenth century Virginia architecture belonged to the English medieval architectural period, which terminated, not in 1558, as often believed, but towards the end of the seventeenth century. Virginia architecture was a direct product, not an "afterglow," of the Middle Ages.

If the reader had sailed up the James River between the time James Fort was founded in 1607 and the year 1620, when the Pilgrim Fathers landed at Plymouth, he would have caught a glimpse of a great variety of structures, practically all erected in the manner of the Middle Ages. From the deck he would have descried along the low banks of Jamestown Island the palisaded fortification, adorned with great timber blockhouses and surrounded by moats. He would have seen, further, town and country houses with walled-in gardens and orchards, called "hortyards"; tobacco barns, corn houses, servants' quarters, storehouses, and warehouses. He would have discerned churches, windmills, sawmills, bloomeries or iron ore furnaces, glassworks, guest houses (inns), taverns, alehouses, stores, shops, silk houses, courts of guard (guard houses), public granaries, tenements and wharves, called "bridges." If he were fortunate, he might have ascended James River far enough to visit Henricopolis and the East India School and the College.[1]

The greater part of these Virginia fabrics were constructed in *at least* five different medieval methods. The visitor would have noted the Anglo-Saxon type of palisade, employed not only for the walls of fortifications and blockhouses, and even churches, but also for plantation houses. The earliest church on Eastern Shore, for instance, possessed palisaded walls much in the manner of the little Saxon church of Greenstead in Essex, England, believed to have been erected in 1013. The vertical timbers, or palings, were stuck in the ground in both examples, like the stake fence of Chaucer's poor widow.

Other freshly built edifications comprised mere board-roofed cottages of puncheons, called "punches" for short — a second medieval method where posts are set a few inches apart in the ground and the panels between the posts are filled with "wattle-

---

[1] Compiled from Kingsbury (1933).

and-daubing." Our modern lath-and-plastering is the direct descendant of this wattling method whereby twigs and branches are plastered on both sides with rough clay.

Other structures would have been built in a radically different manner, involving a third medieval method, the "cruck." Certain churches and dwellings were "set on crucks," that is, supported by pairs of bent timbers formed by the split halves of trees. These pairs of bent posts were placed at intervals of one bay, or about sixteen feet apart, according to medieval usage. Walls and roofs were covered with swamp grass and weighted down with earth.

If the visitor arrived in Virginia as early as 1608 or 1609, he would have perceived that some settlers copied Indian fashions by roofing with bark instead of thatch, and by hanging straw mats on the inside. Nevertheless, the Indian methods were the exception — most settlers erecting wattled walls plastered with bitumen, a kind of asphalt, or tough clay, in the approved mode of European antiquity.

At the same time, it would have been recognized that all Virginia constructions were not of such rustic vintage, nor so cottage-like. The traveler would have been impressed by the large number of well-built and substantial timber-framed structures in the earliest years of the Colony. By timber-framed is meant the construction of buildings on a framework of great oaken posts, sills, studs, beams, rafters, and the like, all pegged together. This fourth medieval method was the most popular in England since the sixteenth century, and the colonists adopted it as a favorite. Upon the solid oak framework were fastened wattle-and-daub panels; but sometimes there was brick nogging or other kind of material, like weatherboarding, upon the framing. Such an abode was known as the "fair English" house; and in 1611 Jamestown had two "fair" rows of them, fully two stories and an upper garret, or cornloft, high.

Still a fifth medieval method of building would have been observed by the visitor. This was the "half-and-half" house, the most sophisticated of all the types. The downstairs was brick; the upstairs, making a pleasant contrast, timber-framed.

Most of the edifices carried "country chimneys," where the great hoods and tall flues were manufactured of wattle-and-daub. Naturally, such contraptions were acknowledged fire hazards. The "Welsh" chimneys in Virginia would have perhaps reminded the visitor that wooden chimneys had been usual in England since the fourteenth century. Even today, a wooden chimney is known to exist in a kitchen situated in New Kent County, Virginia.

Although there has been found no record of them, brick dwellings were probably erected before 1620 in the Colony. It would be surprising to discover that Virginians, who had manufactured brick from 1607 onwards, had not put up brick structures in the first thirteen years. Besides, the English had constructed brick edifices since the early thirteenth century.

Now, if the visitor came over to Virginia after the so-called cottage period of the first few years, he would have noticed, as he sailed up and down the verdant-banked tidal rivers, that the architecture was far from uniform in style, and that it bore the stamps of the various shires from which the settlers emigrated. There was no all-embracing type of Virginia house, based, for instance, on the East Anglian cottage, as some writers have stated.[2] Virginians came chiefly from England, and from *every* part of England. As a result, there obtained in this Colony infinite architectural variety. Anything from a "Cornish" farmhouse to a "Yorkshire" manor might catch the eye. Except for minor changes, like tobacco barns — dependencies not seen in England — Virginia architecture was a representative copy of that in the shires across the seas.

In understanding the domestic side of Virginia building, the reader should note that certain differences existed between the town house and that of the country. From earliest years, insofar as present evidence indicates, the urban dwelling was two-stories-and-attic high, as exemplified in 1611 by the two fair rows at James City, and about 1635 by the First State House there. It is not generally known that many abodes followed certain stock dimensions in accordance with English medieval building laws, such as required over-all dimensions of twenty-by-forty or sixteen-by-twenty-four feet. For example, the First State House at Jamestown had a unit floor plan of twenty-by-forty based on the London row house plan. Its gables faced the street in the medieval manner.

Even if it were stylistically more backward in design than the town house, the rural dwelling exemplifies more freedom in design. It seems to have run a course of development from the one-room-and-loft cottage to the great Georgian mansion of the early 1700's. The simplest dwelling was one bay long, or one and a fraction thereof, as illustrated by William May's house at Jamestown and the "House on Isaac Watson's Land." Before its destruction, the Watson lodging appears to have had ingle recesses or chimney pents, medieval features derived from England.

The Adam Thoroughgood House in Princess Anne County, Virginia, perhaps built about 1640, is a good representative of a class of structure once distributed along tidewater. This type is the hall-and-parlor abode, where the "hall," or "great hall," was larger than the parlor. Another example is the Wishart House in Norfolk, Virginia. Such habitations were about twenty feet by forty in size, with gable-end

---

[2] Wertenbaker (1942), pp. 76, 80; Wertenbaker, *Golden Age*, p. 114.

chimneys, either flush or like "pyramids." The stacks were T-shaped in plan, and the dormerless roofs very steep. Little square lie-on-your-stomach windows pierced the gable-end walls, and the principal doors and windows were arched.

The next step in development was to partition off the "hall" in order to make a central passageway— an arrangement instituting the typical Virginia house, such as Pinewoods (Warburton's), the Keeling House, or Kis Kis Kiack.

It was a very simple matter to take either the hall-and-parlor dwelling or the homestead of central passage design, and add an enclosed porch to the front and a wing at the rear. In this manner was formed the cross-house, culmination of rural Virginia architecture in the seventeenth century. Bacon's Castle, with its Jacobean gables and late Gothic "diamond" stacks, is the most noted example. An old woodcut reveals that it had a "curtain" and kitchen wing, a scheme reminiscent of many a seventeenth-century house. In medieval England the curtain appears to have been called "penthouse." Also, over the main doorway of Bacon's Castle was carved in the brick an incipient or embryonic pediment in clumsy Jacobean fashion.

Other examples of the cruciform dwelling in Virginia are the destroyed Fourth State House at Jamestown, with great chimneys uniquely placed on the long sides of the edifice; Malvern Hill, mostly reduced to ashes, but still having an arched brick porch and walls with glazed brick lozenges known as "black diapering"; Foster's Castle, with its casement windows in groups, its bull's-eye window in the porch gable and its "battlemented" doorway; and Christ's Cross, called Criss Cross for short, with its handsome Tudor door and grotesquely carved post.

In the ecclesiastical architecture of Virginia the crossroads church emerges as a distinctive institution. Passing over the first four wooden buildings at James City, we meet with three brick churches of the English Gothic style which are examples of the aisleless nave type. These are the Old Brick Church, called St. Luke's, built in Isle of Wight County probably about 1682, the ruined Jamestown Brick Church of 1647, and the demolished Second Bruton Parish Church, completed in 1683 in Williamsburg. The first two, it seems, were marked by Flemish Gothic gables with "crow steps," and buttresses, pointed arched windows, and bell towers. The third had Jacobean curvilinear gables, a great bull's-eye window, and buttresses. Another sort of church appears to have been represented in Virginia at this time by the "Ace of Clubs," old Pungoteague, which certain gentry, cardplayers it is said, erected cruciformly, with an apse on the eastern arm.

In short, the special characteristics of the Virginia medieval style of architecture, insofar as this style is based on existing brick constructions, may be listed for the sake of convenience as follows. Of course it is evident that all these characteristics do not pertain to one building, but to examples of architecture spread over the whole countryside.

1. *The gables*:

Steeply pointed, usually at a pitch of 54 degrees to the horizon. Occasionally gables faced the street. Chimneys were freestanding, pyramidal, or flush with "setbacks" at the ridge of the roof, or T-shaped in plan, or "diamond" and square. Mousetooth brick courses in the chimney caps.

Not all gables were pointed, however:

Curvilinear gables, called Jacobean, as well as corbie or crow-stepped gables.

Other gable details were the following:

Lie-on-your-stomach windows. Lines of glazed brick following the rake of the roof. Black diapering. The ingle recess or chimney pent.

2. *The façades*:

Segmental-arched windows and doors. Rubbed or gauged flat arches over windows and doors (*post* 1670). Wrought-iron or wooden lattice casement windows, with quarrels and calmes. Mullioned and traceried windows. Board shutters. Unglazed cellar windows with vertical or horizontal square wooden bars, set diagonally in the frame. Battened doors, molded or plain, sometimes nail-studded. Battlemented doorways.

The façades had the following details of brickwork:

Flemish, or checkerboard, bond; or English bond. Chamfered watertable bricks, called "sqynchons." Fancy molded bricks, like the ovolo or the ogee. Brick corbels or brackets to stop the box cornice.

In addition there were sometimes these features on the façades:

Buttresses. Quoins, which were Jacobean. Chimneys on the long sides of the house.

3. *The wings*:

Outshuts, the English name for lean-tos or sheds. Curtains, known as penthouses in medieval times. The enclosed porch or vestibule, having arches or side windows, and benches. The porch chamber above the vestibule. Incipient or embryonic brick pediments of Jacobean design.

One of the most medieval of appendages was:

The stair tower, with winding staircase or stair in straight flights around the walls.

4. *The roofs*:

Covered with shingles, slate, shingle tiles, or pantiles. Little squat, gabled dormer windows, rare (*post* 1690). "Pyramids," or hips.

5. *The interiors*:

Exposed post-and-beam construction. Beamed ceilings, with summer beams, wall plates, and joists. Lambs' tongues and chamfered moldings. Pargetry or ornamental plasterwork on the ceilings. Sometimes fresco.[3] Sloping ceilings in attics.

The walls and floors may be described as follows:

Wainscoting and partitioning with vertical battens, or plain plastered and white-washed walls. Wide plank floors, pegged; or brick floors of English or Dutch brick.[4]

Other features of the interior were:

The great fireplace with oak beam, measuring eight to twelve feet from breast to breast. Delft faïence tiles. The hooded and wooden fireplace. Brick ovens and brew-ing coppers. Shallow closets on either side of the fireplace. The staircase, or boxed-in winding stair, often beside the fireplace. Batten doors with strap hinges, cock's-head hinges, butterfly hinges, H-L hinges, and key escutcheons. Lattice casements with or without elaborate fasteners and latch bars.

All through the eighteenth century, and well into the nineteenth, the medieval tradition continued. The so-called Gothic Revival style of architecture flourished side by side with the true Gothic, and was never aware of its existence. A good way to divide the medieval period in Virginia architecture from the classical Georgian is the introduction of the sash window. This kind of sash was not like ours — that is, double-hung — but a "guillotine." Although the sash window seems to have infiltrated into this Colony in the last decade of the seventeenth century, such a new-fangled inven-tion did not prevent many a settler from hanging on to his accustomed casement window for two or three decades after the year 1700. The passing of the old medieval fashion was very slow.

All the rural types of the medieval period penetrated into the eighteenth century, represented by the Tabb House, Eastwood, Skiff's Creek, and the Custis House, to name four examples out of thousands. But there were transitional sorts of dwellings

---

[3] See Forman (1938), 121.

[4] Hard yellow bricks about 6 inches long are Dutch brick. English statute bricks were made about 9 inches long.

as well; and consequently, there are found here and there instances of structures with a little "cell" or "aisle" along the back, as at Towles Point and Dahl's Swamp. Instead of deepening his home, sometimes the planter merely raised it two full stories, still keeping the medieval narrowness. Ringfield and the Dr. Lucas House are good examples.

Gambrel and hipped-roof dwellings are also transitional. In spite of all the transitional specimens cropping up throughout the Virginia countryside in the first half of the eighteenth century, the great tradition of the Middle Ages was the stronger. Even the dependencies and certain important features of the main houses of the great Georgian plantations in Virginia could not escape the influence of the earlier age. The time-honored building methods and designing fashions of previous centuries moved forward through the eighteenth century, and into the next, like a flood tide that cannot be easily slowed.

145. TOWLES POINT, LANCASTER COUNTY, VIRGINIA
Built about 1711, this house has ingle recesses and little back rooms or cells.

146. GUNN'S RUN, CHARLES CITY COUNTY, VIRGINIA
An eighteenth-century cottage, showing persistence of medieval style. The left-hand wing was probably built first.

147. THE BRICK STATE HOUSE OF 1676, ST. MARY'S CITY, MARYLAND

The great Assembly Hall in this reconstructed building has the open-beam ceiling, brick floor, and casement windows typical of the Middle Ages.

PART III

Maryland Medieval Architecture

I

CASTLE AND COT IN OLD ST. MARY'S CITY

IN EARLY Maryland there was practiced the greatest measure of religious and civic freedom hitherto known in the Americas.[1] The first proprietor of this colony, Cecilius Calvert, second Lord Baltimore, held a deep-seated preference for a province where Protestant and Roman Catholic could live together peaceably in that intolerant age. The original settlement and capital [2] of Maryland, St. Mary's City, located on a branch of the Potomac River about eighty miles below the city of Washington, marks the spot where religious freedom was for the first time recognized as a policy of government. Also it was in this bygone town, now almost wholly buried under green meadows, that the medieval architecture of Maryland first began to flourish.

Perhaps because of this very latitude in devotional and governmental matters, there was introduced a certain amount of freedom in architectural design. It is believed that there was a greater range of house types in Maryland than in Virginia at this period.

It is unfortunate that most Americans, if they have heard of the place at all, hold misconceptions about the size and appearance of St. Mary's City. For example, the writer was once informed by an inhabitant of a northern state that she thought St. Mary's City comprised a collection of shacks or log cabins. The very reverse was true. At the time that Plymouth in Massachusetts was a village of wooden cabins, St. Mary's (c. 1640) had many a two-story brick edifice, including the largest residence built in the American Colonies by Englishmen. It is probable that the Maryland capital was even more imposing than Jamestown.

It is true that for the first two or three years after the establishment of St. Mary's in 1634 the early colonists lived in "cottages" of flimsy materials. One of the most prominent settlers, Thomas Cornwaleys, wrote in 1638 that he was "building of A house toe put my head in, of sawn Timber framed, A story and half hygh, with A seller and Chimnies of brick toe Encourage others toe follow my Example, for hitherto wee Live in Cottages." [3]

[1] Andrews (1934–38), II, 190.   [2] From 1634 to 1694.   [3] *Calvert Papers*, no. 1, p. 174.

Among the early timber-framed structures in the city was the Calvert House, or East St. Mary's, "a large framd house," erected in 1634, or soon after, by the governor, Leonard Calvert. The Court of Guard and the storehouse within the square palisade must have been wooden, as well as the mill set up on the edge of town for the grinding of corn. In spite of the fact that historians seem to unite in designating these early structures log cabins or log houses, there are no references before 1660 to such huts in Maryland.[4]

Within five years after its settlement St. Mary's City possessed a number of brick edifices, of which three are worthy of note: the Chapel of St. Mary's, a Gothic Church described in a later chapter; the Palace of St. John's, first "palace," so-called, in the Colonies, with a roof covered with medieval pantiles; and St. Peter's, popularly known as the Governor's Castle (Fig. 148), of which our excavations have revealed something of the original appearance.[5]

It is a rare thing to find in the period of the early settlements a structure which was significant equally from an historical and an architectural viewpoint. The Governor's Castle was the most historic dwelling of seventeenth-century Maryland, since it served as the home of Charles, Lord Baltimore, second proprietor of the province, and as the home of the first royal governors. The mansion had, as far as is known, the largest floor area of any residence built by Englishmen on the shores of the New World by the end of the year 1639. It was the largest house of its time in the Colonies. The only known larger contemporary structure was Harvard College, made of wood and completed some five years after the Castle.[6] Besides, there is no other floor scheme of the period in this country even remotely resembling that of the Castle.

Its builder was Thomas Cornwaleys, the settler who previously had set up a timber-framed house in which to put his head. By May of 1640 the dwelling later known as the Governor's Castle was described as a brick house having been lately set up. After Cornwaleys returned to England, the chancellor of Maryland lived there, and the habitation became known as the "Chancellor's House at St. Peter's." In 1682, Charles Calvert, third Lord Baltimore, was the next occupant, and in 1691, the royal governor, Sir Lionel Copley, is believed to have been tenant there. After Copley came Sir Edmond Andros and Sir Francis Nicholson.

In appearance the Castle was a massive, square edifice of dark brick, two stories high, with walls penetrated by narrow, lattice casement windows (Figs. 148, 150).

---

[4] *Maryland Archives,* I, 490. See Forman (1938), p. 197.

[5] Excavations in 1940 aided by a grant awarded by the American Council of Learned Societies, Washington.

[6] Morison (1935), p. 272.

148. THE GOVERNOR'S CASTLE, ST. MARY'S CITY, MARYLAND, 1639

A reconstruction drawing of the largest house of its time in the American colonies. In 1694 the Castle blew up.

CASTLE AND COTTAGE IN EARLIEST MARYLAND

149. Timber-framed State House of 1664, St. Mary's City, Maryland, projected but never erected. Block floor plan.

150. The Governor's Castle, or St. Peter's, St. Mary's City, Maryland, 1639. Reconstruction of floor plan and side elevation (approximate). Compare with Figs. 148, 151. (After Forman, 1942)

151. Gatley Park, Aymestry, England, c. 1630–40. Floor plan at small scale. Compare with Fig. 150. (After *Herefordshire*, III)

152. Richard Wright's dwelling, Maryland, c. 1658. (Reconstruction drawings of block floor plan and perspective by author after description in *Maryland Archives*)

153. Resurrection Manor, St. Mary's County, Maryland, c. 1660. The original, one-room-and-loft house. Compare with Fig. 162.

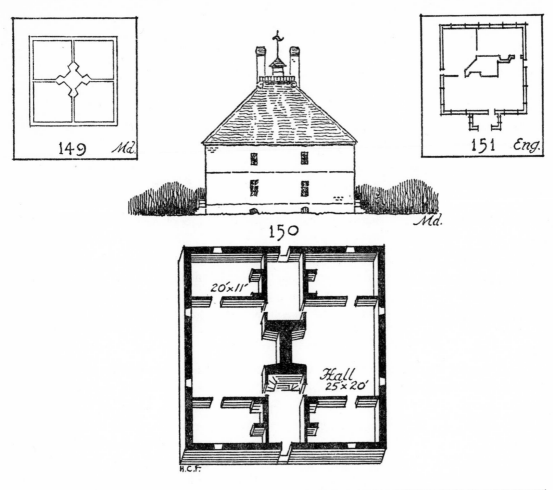

149   *Md.*

150

Md.

151   *Eng.*

20′×11′

Hall
25′×20′

H.C.F.

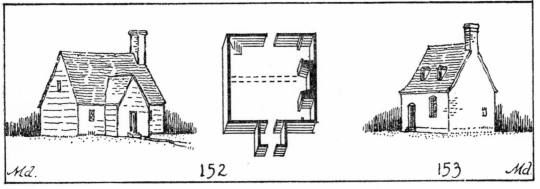

Md.   152   153   *Md.*

According to accounts, the roof was crowned by a wooden balustraded parapet, which terminated at each corner in a scroll like the head of a violin, and supported in the middle a kind of "entablature." This "entablature" was evidently a cupola, and it boasted a weathercock. Near the middle of the house stood two stout chimneys, which appear to have risen — so the exigencies of the floor plan required — at the front and back of the parapet, in such a manner that a traveler approaching the main entrance would be unable to see the rear chimney, because of the one in front. The roof itself was laid with "plain" or "shingle" tiles of a size approximately conforming to the medieval specifications of a statute of 1477 in the time of Edward IV.[7]

The Castle was exactly square. It measured fifty-four feet on a side and had a room of equal size in each corner. Such square-shaped blocks were built in England in Jacobean times and are exemplified by Bolsover Castle, built in 1613 in Derbyshire, or Clegg Hall, of 1620, in Lancashire. Gatley Park (Fig. 151), erected in Hereford-shire about 1630–40, has a floor scheme akin to that of the Governor's Castle.

In front of the Maryland edifice was a grassy courtyard, shut in by a sweep of wall, through which admission was gained by a heavy iron gate, ten feet wide, swung between square, stuccoed pillars, each of which was surmounted by a couchant lion carved in stone.

It is a great misfortune that the Castle was blown up by gunpowder in the first week of October, 1694. Sir Francis Nicholson, later founder of Williamsburg in Virginia, was supposed to have been dwelling in the building at the time, but he escaped the accident. No one knows who were the malefactors, or who kept seventeen barrels of gunpowder in the great basement. For the next hundred years the Castle crumbled, until today there is nothing to show for that vast pile but a tobacco field.

The design of the Castle perhaps was to have been reflected in a timber-framed State House (Fig. 149), which was ordered to be built in 1664 in St. Mary's City, but which never passed the condition of "castle in the air." It was to be forty feet square, two and a half stories high, with a "tamett" or cupola in the center. There was to be a cellar under part of the house, and also a twelve-foot wing. Each floor of the main part was to have four rooms, one fireplace to each.

It may be that the design of the Governor's Castle was reflected in the great brick Governor's Palace in Williamsburg, erected three quarters of a century later. There are several similarities between them. But that is another story.[8]

[7] See Forman (1938), p. 90. Size of shingle tile: 10½″ x 6¼″ x ⅝″.
[8] Forman (1942).

II

THE MARYLAND HOUSE TRANSPLANTED
FROM ENGLAND

IN seventeenth-century Maryland the country house was either a manor house or a plantation house. The provincial manor was a true one, that is, it comprised a landed estate of the thousand-acre class, along with legal privileges, exactly like the courts-leet and courts-baron of medieval England. Consequently, there was in Maryland not only a medieval style of architecture, but also a feudal system deeply ingrained in the social and political structure.

On the other hand, the manor dwelling in the Free State was in appearance not similar to the imposing amplitude of the English manor, but small and relatively insignificant. It was more like the English cottage than anything else.

To all intents and purposes the early houses were, as we have already seen in the case of Virginia, transplanted English ones. In truth, some of the Maryland seats were unbelievably puny, like Henry Potter's ten-foot dwelling-house of 1652.[1] Another settler, Paul Simpson, is reported to have constructed an abode fifteen feet square. In 1656, the fifteen-foot dwelling of another colonist cost him three hundred pounds of tobacco, the currency in those days. In Charles County, one James Linsey erected a house twenty feet long. A Deputy Governor and Commissioner of Lord Baltimore's Treasury by the name of James Neale lived in 1661 in a wooden structure, Wolleston Manor, which was declared to be only twenty-five feet in length.[2] It was a rare example of Maryland architecture that reached an extent of fifty feet.

So small were the early dwellings that the third Lord Baltimore, after sailing up and down the tidal rivers, reported that the houses were "very meane and Little, and generally after the manner of the meanest farm houses in England." Such a picture strengthens our visualization of the strong Gothic character of the Maryland home. The meanest farmhouses in seventeenth-century England were fashioned in the medieval style.

In keeping with the country dwellings of Virginia, and with the ancient rural seats

[1] *Maryland Archives*, X, 197.
[2] *Maryland Archives*, X, 301, 302; LIII, 26, 27; XLI, 526; LI, 71.

of the mother country, the Maryland lodging usually carried with it a flock of out-houses. For instance, Snow Hill Manor in 1639 possessed among other dependencies a store, corn loft, servants' lodge, and hogsties. Other plantations had tobacco houses, slave quarters, hen houses, smoke houses, spinning houses, stables, granaries, dairies, blacksmith shops, and offices. Most of these outbuildings were for the most part strewn about in unsymmetrical order, as in England. Of course, tobacco huts had no counterpart abroad; but they were built with eaves low to the ground and with great posts and beams in the style of the Middle Ages. It is curious to discover that most tobacco barns in Maryland were larger than manor houses. For example, Robert Brooke, acting governor in 1652, had two "great houses full of tobacco: the one 100 ft in length the other 90 ft."

How medieval in appearance were the early homes may be gauged by the number of "Welsh" or wooden country chimneys extant in those days (Fig. 9). The Maryland landscape, like the Virginian, was one of wooden stacks. As has been described,[3] the Welsh chimney is a wicker and thatch affair, still to be seen in Carmarthenshire and on the English side of the Welsh border. It comprised a hood or canopy of wattle-and-daub, or lath-and-plaster, set over the fire. In 1400 practically all dwellings in Britain had frame chimneys, and the fire hazard was enormous. Accordingly, it cannot come to us as a surprise that, in Maryland, Paul Simpson's house, fifteen feet square, possessed a "welch Chimney."[4] The framework of such a configuration was of wooden posts, as is proved by reference to James Hall's twenty-foot homestead at Hebden's Point, Calvert County. Hall was required to "putt up the Posts of the Welch Chimney." In 1685 in St. Mary's City housekeepers were ordered to have all their chimneys "lathed, filled, daubed and playstered," and to have two ladders, twelve and twenty-four feet long respectively, provided for each chimney.[5] It also appears that old Cecil Friends' Meetinghouse, built about 1696 on the Eastern Shore, had a similar hood, described as an "Inside hanging Chimly."

While no square or diamond stacks, such as crowned the chimneys of Bacon's Castle and the Matthew Jones House in Virginia, have been discovered in Maryland, we know that there were many examples of this kind of chimney stack in the Province. The Piney Neck House, built in 1642 in St. Mary's County by Governor Leonard Calvert, had a stack of brick chimneys, containing two flues, in the middle of the manor. Another edifice had "two stacks of brick chimneys."

The more the seventeenth-century habitation is studied, the more convincing becomes the proof of its medieval flavor. Note, for example, the twenty-five-foot square

[3] See Part II, Chapter II.
[4] *Maryland Archives*, X, 278.
[5] Annapolis, Deeds, Liber WRC1, folios 459 to 463.

frame dwelling of Richard Wright, dating from 1658 (Fig. 152). The main room downstairs was called the "hall," in the English manner. The stairs were "sealed," that is, set in a box in approved medieval style. Further, there was a little enclosed "porch," with windows in the sides, much in the manner of the ancient vestibules of England and Virginia.

The leaded casement, too, was found everywhere in the early days of the Province. Recent excavations have revealed that St. Mary's City was once full of casement windows, and references to structures in other parts of the Colony indicate their prevalence. For example, the first two County Court Houses in Talbot County possessed these Gothic features. When the roof of Snow Hill Manor blew off in 1639, twenty-eight feet of glass was employed for the repair of the windows, as well as an abundant supply of lead solder for mending the lead strips of the casements. Recently, existing wooden casements with diamond panes have been discovered in the walls of the old wing of Holly Hill in Anne Arundel County.

It is known that four of the five medieval methods of wall construction employed in earliest Virginia were common to Maryland. The St. Mary's Fort of 1634 used the first method, palisading or vertical posts set side by side in the earth. The Talbot County jail on Wye River appears to have had the second method, puncheoning, where the square posts were placed four inches apart in the ground and were then covered with clapboards or weatherboarding. No Maryland record so far discovered mentions the third method, the cruck, like that used at James City in 1607; but, at least, the Province had the roof-thatching peculiar to such a structure: witness the "Thatcht" house standing in 1656 in Kent County on Eastern Shore.[6]

The fourth method, timber-framing, known as the "oak" tradition, which came into use in Virginia in 1611 or earlier, was common to Maryland in the days of its founding. There were, and still are, dwellings framed by means of "posts," "groundsills," "wallplates," "summer" beams, "small joists," and "girders." It is the method in practice today for wooden houses erected by American carpenters, and it harks back to England for centuries.

The fifth and last method was what we have called the "half-and-half" work, where the first floor was wholly brick, and the second story timber-framed. Birmingham Manor, the destroyed Snowden homestead in Anne Arundel County, Maryland, was a good example (Fig. 205). In England a comparable structure is Saint Aylotts, Saffron Walden, Essex, built about 1500, "the lower storey of brick . . . the upper timber-framed."[7]

[6] *Maryland Archives*, LIV, 86.
[7] *Essex* I, 242.

MEDIEVAL TOWN HOUSES IN MARYLAND, AND COMPARATIVE COUNTRY HOUSE PLANS SHOWING DEVELOPMENT

154. Two row houses in St. Mary's City, Maryland, traditionally believed to have been the Secretary's Office or Council Chamber, c. 1664. (Reconstruction drawing after Forman, 1938)

155. Block plan of the above.

156. Two row houses in St. Mary's City, Maryland, known as "A town house within the Fort." Probably c. 1634–1638. Erroneously known as Smith's Town House. (Reconstruction)

157. The Ending of Controversie, Talbot County, Maryland, c. 1670, partly destroyed. Example of hall-and-parlor type. Compare with Fig. 168. (After Forman, 1939)

158. Make Peace, Somerset County, Maryland, c. 1663. Example of central-passage type. Compare with Fig. 170. (After Forman, 1934)

159. Cotswold cottage at Tunley, near Sapperton, Gloucestershire, England, showing hall-and-parlor type. Compare with Fig. 157. (After Oliver, 1929)

160. Brick State House of 1676, St. Mary's City, Maryland. An example of the cross type. Compare with Fig. 180. (After Forman, 1938)

161. Leigh House, on St. Mary's Hill Freehold, St. Mary's City, Maryland. The original one-room-and-loft dwelling. (After Forman, 1938)

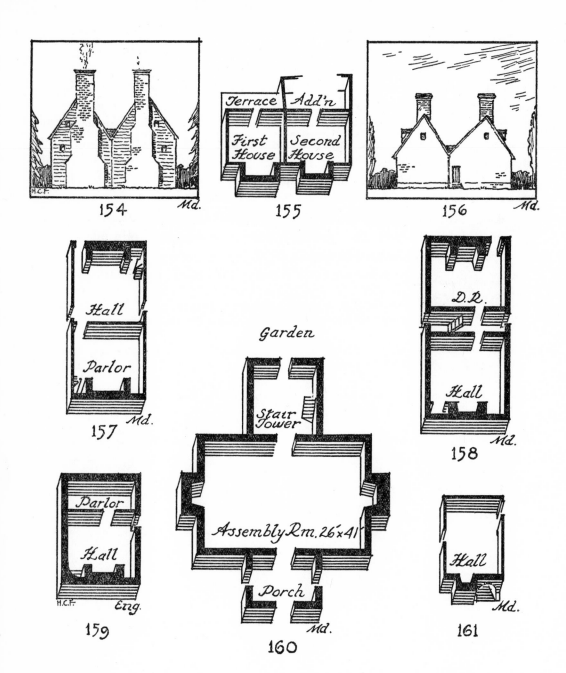

154

155

Terrace Add'n

First House Second House

156

Hall

Parlor

157

Garden

Stair Tower

D.R.

Hall

158

Parlor

Hall

159

Assembly Rm. 26'×41'

Porch

160

Hall

161

A variety of the "half-and-half" house is that dwelling which has a mixture of wooden and brick walls. Sometimes one, two, or even three walls were of brick; and of course this method gave the walls a pleasant contrast in texture. In Calvert County, Upper Bennett has one brick wall, a gable end; Clocker's Fancy (Fig. 161) in St. Mary's City carries both gables of brick; and demolished Carthagena (Fig. 203) on St. Mary's River possessed three sides of the house of brick — a unique specimen. At the same time it should not be forgotten that this particular kind of "half-and-half" cottage prevailed in Great Britain in the Middle Ages, where there are numerous specimens extant, notably a dwelling at Hurst Green, Sussex,[8] and the Cradle House, Marksall, Essex.[9]

Taking one thing with another, the Maryland dwelling of the seventeenth century was a transplanted English one. Naturally, there were differences of a minor sort; but the similarities were overwhelming.

[8] Dawber (1900), pl. 93.
[9] *Essex*, III, 177.

III

THE TOWN HOUSE OF THE EARLY MARYLANDER

UPON THE founding of Maryland, Cecilius Calvert, second Lord Baltimore, gave instructions for the laying out of the City of St. Mary's, and for the erection of town dwellings. All planters, he commanded, were to erect their homes in as decent and uniform a manner as their own "endowments" and the site of the settlement afforded. Further, the dwellings were to be near "adioning one to another" — in other words, row houses. What ineptitude to give a bureaucratic order like this one, which could not be, and was not, carried out! It is true that an attempt was made to construct city houses in rows in Maryland, as was done at Jamestown under the King's orders; yet, after all is said and done, very little came of it. Inasmuch as Englishmen possessed nearly half a continent in which to spread out, why should they have cramped their houses?

There have been discovered so far in Maryland the remains of only two pairs of row houses, and these once stood along Aldermanbury Street in St. Mary's City. One pair, known at this writing as "A town house within the Fort"[1] (Fig. 156), was by a curious coincidence exactly the same size as the First State House at Jamestown. Both measured sixty-seven and a half feet by forty. The plan of the Maryland edifice is, however, unique in America. Our archaeological investigation[2] shows that the north part was erected first with back-to-back fireplaces. A passageway extending the whole length of the structure was next added on the south. Finally, an addition similar in size and shape to the original structure was attached to the passageway. In the ruins of the pile was discovered the first piece of leaded glass, or quarrel, found in the state, indicating the former use of lattice casements.

The other pair of row buildings was a structure now identified tentatively as the Secretary's Office or the Council Chamber (Figs. 154, 155). It was probably the first Maryland House of Records. The order of 1664 for the erection of a Secretary's Office called for a timber-framed dwelling, twenty feet square, two and a half stories

[1] Hitherto erroneously identified as "Smith's Town House."
[2] Forman (1938), chapter xviii.

high, with a brick chimney. Excavations of the ruins seem to have confirmed this size and substance; and also the remains of another twenty-by-twenty addition were brought to light.

As far as is known, the Secretary's Office had the largest fireplace of its time in Maryland. It was a little room in itself, measuring ten feet by four feet eight inches. The size of the red "Dutch" bricks employed in the construction of this fireplace corresponds exactly to that of the "Dutch" bricks in the England of the Middle Ages, as at fifteenth-century Tattershall Castle.[3]

But it is not in the town house of early Maryland that medieval architecture can be viewed best — so few are the known examples. One must turn, perforce, to the rural dwellings, of which more than a hundred specimens exist today.

[3] Lloyd (1928), pp. 4ff.

IV

THE EVOLUTION OF THE MEDIEVAL COUNTRY HOUSE IN MARYLAND

BEGINNING in 1634, and continuing through the century, the country house evolved from the elementary one-room-and-attic cottage to the stately residence of the eighteenth century. Of course, it cannot be laid down as the rule that all the plain, simple structures were built first, and all the complicated ones later. On the other hand, the situation was much like that in Virginia: homes with more than two rooms and passageway were generally built in late seventeenth-century times.

The first type, the elementary cottage, was very prevalent in Maryland in the early days. In fact it was the equivalent of Bishop Hall's English hut of one bay's breadth ("God wot!"). A bay, as we have already seen, was about sixteen feet, and the reverend bishop called the one-bay shelter a "silly cote whose thatched sparres are furr'd with sluttish soote a whole inch thick." It is a pity that no known seventeenth-century example of a one-bay house stands today in Maryland. However, the original portions of the Leigh House in St. Mary's City, of Resurrection Manor (Fig. 153) in St. Mary's County, and of Holly Hill in Anne Arundel County, conformed to this elementary type.

The Leigh House (Figs. 161, 167),[1] possibly dating from the 1650's, had three sides of wood and one gable end brick. It was small in size, measuring only fourteen feet by twenty. A cellar, lighted by diminutive barred windows in the medieval manner, gave extra space for the tenant. The joists of the floor were oak trees, with the bark still upon them after nearly three hundred years. It is interesting to note that the chimney is what is known as a "freestanding" or "offset" one, because the stack stood clear of the gable wall in order to lessen the risk of fire. In England of the Middle Ages the origin of the freestanding chimney was due to the need to keep the flue away from inflammable thatched eaves.

The earliest part of Holly Hill (Fig. 249), built about 1667 in Anne Arundel County, was a one-room-and-loft dwelling of walnut sills, oak studs, oak rafters, and

---

[1] Incorrectly called St. Peter's Key in Forman (1938), chapter 20.

MEDIEVAL MARYLAND DWELLINGS

162. Resurrection Manor, or Scotch Neck, St. Mary's County, Maryland, c. 1660. On the façade the line of the addition on the left may be seen. Compare with Fig. 153.

163. Clocker's Fancy, St. Mary's City, Maryland, c. 1658.

164. Wye House, Talbot County, Maryland, c. 1662. The original brick cottage having chimney stack with a "withe."

165. Clay's Neck, Talbot County, Maryland, c. 1679; destroyed 1935. (Reconstruction)

166. Long Lane Farm, St. Mary's County, Maryland, c. 1670. The original portion, with free-standing chimneys. (Forman, 1934)

167. Leigh House, on St. Mary's Hill Freehold, St. Mary's City, Maryland, c. 1650 (?). The original one-story-and-loft cottage. Compare with Fig. 161. (After Forman, 1938)

162

163   164   165

166   167

MORE MEDIEVAL MARYLAND DWELLINGS

168. The Ending of Controversie, Talbot County, Maryland, c. 1670, partly destroyed. Had brick gables and palisade construction. Compare with Fig. 157. (After Forman, 1939)

169. Springfield, Kent County, Maryland, late seventeenth century. (After Forman, 1934, and field notes)

170. Make Peace, Somerset County, Maryland, c. 1663. West and east gables, showing black diapering. Compare with Fig. 158. (After Forman, 1934)

171. Calvert's Rest, St. Mary's County, Maryland, c. 1661. Original appearance of brick gable.

172. Preston, sometimes called Charles' Gift, Calvert County, Maryland, 1652. Casements reconstructed. (After Forman, 1934)

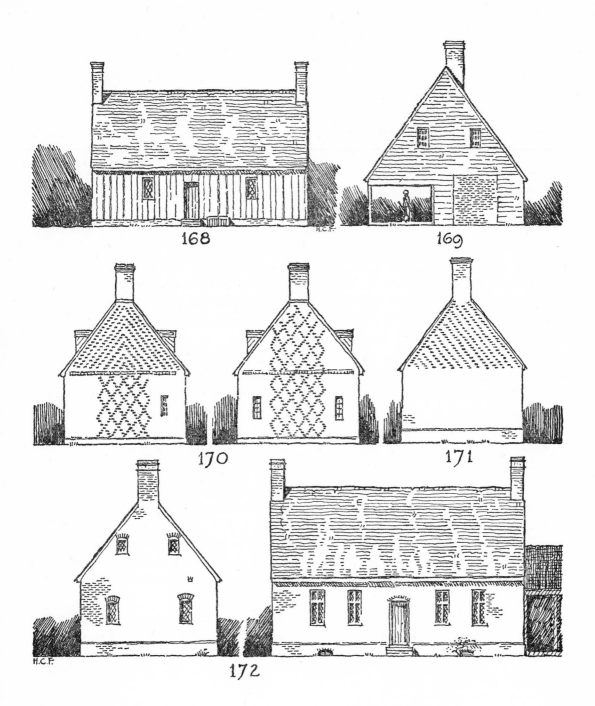

168

169

170

171

172

oak clapboards. The chimney was a tremendous "pyramid," and the windows were casements with diamond panes.

When the Maryland planter became a little wealthier, or had a larger family, he added another room, as was done at Holly Hill between 1667 and 1700, thus forming a "hall-and-parlor" house. In such examples the hall was always larger than the parlor. Now it so happens that several of the oldest dwellings of Maryland belong to this classification. Besides Holly Hill, they are Clocker's Fancy, Preston, Resurrection Manor, Parrott's Cage, and the early portions of Long Lane Farm and Mansion Hall — all standing in southern Maryland; and The Ending of Controversie, Clay's Neck, Mulberry Grove and Wye House, located on Eastern Shore. Brief descriptions of these survivals will aid the reader to form a general picture of this kind of dwelling — a type which at one time prevailed on the banks of all the chief rivers of Maryland.

In St. Mary's City stands Clocker's Fancy (Fig. 163), built, we believe, about 1658 by Daniel Clocker I. An excellent example of the hall-and-parlor dwelling, it has brick gables and timber-framed sides, insulated with brick nogging. The steep staircase beside one of the fireplaces winds its way by nine continuous winders and three straight steps from the hall to the little east bedroom in the loft, originally lit, not by dormers, but by lie-on-your-stomach windows.

Winding staircases, or "sealed" stairs, are English medieval constructions. A staircase, for instance, at Wardes Otham, Kentshire, of 1370,[2] rises from an open-roofed hall in five winders, thereupon turns in the opposite direction to form an S-curve. In Galehouse Farm, Felstead, Essex, is another winding staircase of about the same period, set close against the chimney in the manner of that at Clocker's Fancy. In sixteenth-century cottages the winding staircase was recurrent. Old Cotswold dwellings (Fig. 159), for example, have very narrow winders ascending from the side of the open fireplace.[3]

For all that, the winding staircase was not the earliest method of reaching the attic. At first, the loft was gained by a "stee" or ladder, and many of these are extant in England. Both great medieval halls and little dwellings of the yeoman employed the ladder.[4]

The second example of the hall-and-parlor abode is brick Preston, sometimes called Charles' Gift (Fig. 172), in Calvert County, Maryland. It was the capitol of the Province in the year 1654. In size it is forty-six feet by twenty-four and a half —

[2] Oswald (1933), p. 24.
[3] Broadbent (1931), pp. 10, 12.
[4] Addy, chapter iii; Braun (1940), pp. 19, 63.

that is, three bays in length. Originally it had two chief rooms, the hall and the parlor, each heated by a capacious arched fireplace. Connected to the main house by a curtain or passageway was a kitchen wing (Fig. 101, *left*). Such a curtain, employed at Bacon's Castle in Virginia, was, as we have already seen, known in medieval England as a penthouse.

Other habitations of this category in southern Maryland are brick Resurrection Manor, a building probably dating from the 1660's and owned at one time by the son of the Earl of Albion, in which the division in the brick walls where the parlor was added can still be traced (Fig. 162); Parrott's Cage, in Calvert County, facetiously named for the builder, William Parrott (c. 1652); Upper Bennett, constructed about 1658 in the same county on land owned and named for Governor Richard Bennett of Virginia; the original portion of Long Lane Farm, Lieutenant John Jarboe's half-and-half lodging (Fig. 166), dating from about 1670, in St. Mary's County; and the earlier part of Mansion Hall, a wooden cottage of the Gray family built perhaps about 1690, in Charles County.

Of these last, Mansion Hall deserves most to engage the reader's attention. Paradoxically, the dwelling is a miniature hall-and-parlor house, and is named "hall" only because of the English connotation. While exploring the vast wooded tracts of Charles County, the writer accidentally discovered Mansion Hall. There are the little medieval lie-on-your-stomach windows, two panes wide, in the gables (Fig. 222), the batten doors, the low ceilings, and the winding staircase of the period. Here, too, was the first Jacobean staircase found in Maryland (Fig. 173) — a stair with as much Jacobean character as the curvilinear gables of Bacon's Castle in Virginia. There is a shaped finial upon a square newel post. The handrail is carved with Gothic moldings, and the balusters are splat- or flat-shaped, cut with a tool like a jigsaw.

This kind of stair to all intents and purposes marks the intermediate step between the Gothic winding sealed stairs and the open Georgian stairway. The splat balusters of Mansion Hall are flat balusters cut to give strange effects, and coeval examples in England are found in the late fifteenth-century gatehouse, Lower Brockhampton, Herefordshire; [5] sixteenth-century Breccles Hall (Fig. 178), Norfolkshire; and early seventeenth-century Manor Farm, Little Hereford.[6] Newel posts did not appear in humble English dwellings until about 1600. A square newel with shaped finial, like that at Mansion Hall in Maryland, can be found at Gillow Manor, Hentland, Herefordshire, of late sixteenth-century date.

On the Eastern Shore of Maryland there were, and still are, other hall-and-parlor

---

[5] *Herefordshire*, II, pl. 39.   [6] *Herefordshire*, III, pl. 73.

dwellings. Of these the most significant was The Ending of Controversie, erected about 1670 by Wenlocke Christison, or Christopherson, in Talbot County (Figs. 157, 168). When the writer last visited the place, it was in the final stage of dilapidation; at this writing all traces of it may have disappeared. Until its destruction the house stood as an unknown monument to the great tradition of religious freedom in the Free State. For, back of this cottage with the unusual name hangs a tale. Because of his Quaker faith, Wenlocke Christison in 1656 suffered twenty-seven "cruel" stripes from the authorities at Plymouth, Massachusetts. There is an interesting story on record about his adventure,[7] but it is sufficient to state here that after being buffeted in the Old World and in the New, he sought the religious sanctuary of Maryland, and built a dwelling-house there. Some say that it was appropriately named by him The Ending of Controversie, but the facts prove otherwise.

In its brick gables and frame sides this habitation resembled Clocker's Fancy. It had the characteristics of the period: great fireplaces, large enough to take a seven-foot log; two "breakneck" winding staircases beside the chimneys; vertical board partitions with simple carved moldings; tiny bedrooms tucked away under the eaves; little lie-on-your-stomach windows. Unlike Clocker's Fancy, however, the side walls carried, not the customary clapboards or weatherboards, but vertical planks, in the manner of English medieval palisading (Figs. 168, 189). The random-width boards were nailed vertically to the sills and studs, and had chamfered strips over the joints in order to keep out the weather. In England the same kind of wall construction appears in the screens of fifteenth-century Haddon Hall (Fig. 191), and in the south porch of All Saints Parish Church, dating from 1663, in Stock, Essex. Of course such a method of placing planks or rough boards upright side by side bespeaks the Anglo-Saxon tradition of palisades, examples of which flourished in earliest Virginia and Maryland, as has been described already.

Like the outside woodwork, the interior wainscoting at Christison's is medieval (Figs. 188, 190). In Kent, England, partition boards in the fifteenth and sixteenth centuries were set up vertically and overlapped one another, in exactly the manner of those in The Ending of Controversie. In another part of England, Westmorland,[8] the local type of wooden partition was much the same: heavy battens or boards alternately molded and plain, extending all the way from the floor to the ceiling. Walls constructed in this way were called "muntin and plank" partitions.

Also on Eastern Shore was Clay's Neck (Fig. 165), built soon after 1679 by Henry Clay, in Talbot County. This was another example of hall-and-parlor cottage

[7] Forman (1939).   [8] *Westmorland*, pl. 59.

with brick ends and lie-on-your-stomach windows. In the same county is another specimen, the original brick Wye House, a Lloyd home of 1662, noted for its chimney of medieval style (Figs. 164, 246). At the ridge level the chimney is offset; and on the front face of the stack a vertical "withe," or projecting row of bricks, marks optically the division between flues, as may be seen in the illustration. Medieval chimneys with withes, like those at Petworth in Sussex (Fig. 247), or Brinscome in Surrey, are common in England.[9]

From the hall-and-parlor house, as in Virginia, the dwelling of central-passage type was formed; yet there are relatively few central-passage homes in Maryland which can be dated in the seventeenth century. Old brick Make Peace, erected about 1663 in Somerset County, is perhaps the best specimen (Figs. 158, 170). It is known as the most southerly colonial house in the state, and at one time was surrounded by a high brick wall as a protection against Indians. So scant is the passageway, measuring only five and a half feet in width, that if you tripped, your head would strike the opposite wall. The six-foot fireplace in the hall is arched like that at Preston in Calvert County. The kitchen, still existing, was at one time a separate building. Like the patterns on the walls of the Keeling House in Virginia, the east gable has "chevrons" or inverted-V designs in glazed brick. On the other gable is "black diapering" of diamond designs (Fig. 81) from ground to ridge.

Other examples of the central-passage type are the original wooden manor-house, My Lord's Gift, constructed soon after 1658 by Colonel Henry DeCourcy in Queen Anne's County; Pasquahanza, of 1680, in Charles County, a little elongated frame cottage with a boxed stair in the passage. Still another was Jutland, supposed to have been the original St. Elizabeth's Manor, in St. Mary's County.

An interesting variation of the central-passage class is Calvert's Rest (Fig. 171), a story-and-loft brick house erected soon after 1661 by William Calvert, son of the first Governor of Maryland. It is located in St. Mary's County. The narrow passage, instead of running across the middle of the habitation, extends the whole length of one long side. In keeping with what has been already stated, there was a certain amount of freedom in architectural design in this province, and Calvert's Rest serves as a good illustration.

[9] Holme (1915), p. 25; Green (1908), pl. 10, 11.

THE JACOBEAN INFLUENCE IN MARYLAND AND ENGLAND

173. Mansion Hall, Charles County, Maryland, late seventeenth century. Slat balusters and newel post with finial. Note Gothic moldings on hand-rail section, *a*.

174. Bond Castle, Calvert County, Maryland, late seventeenth century, now destroyed. Curvilinear door head to entrance vestibule. Compare with Fig. 175.

175. Pitchford Hall, Shropshire, England. Curvilinear door head. (After Tipping)

176. Holly Hill, Anne Arundel County, Maryland, c. 1730. Curvilinear window head with carved keys. Compare with Figs. 177 and 249.

177. Pallant House, Chichester, England, c. 1713. Curvilinear window head with carved keys. (After Lloyd, 1925)

178. Breccles Hall, Norfolk, England. Slat balusters. (After Tipping)

179. Brandy, Anne Arundel County, Maryland, early nineteenth century. Curvilinear board on porch.

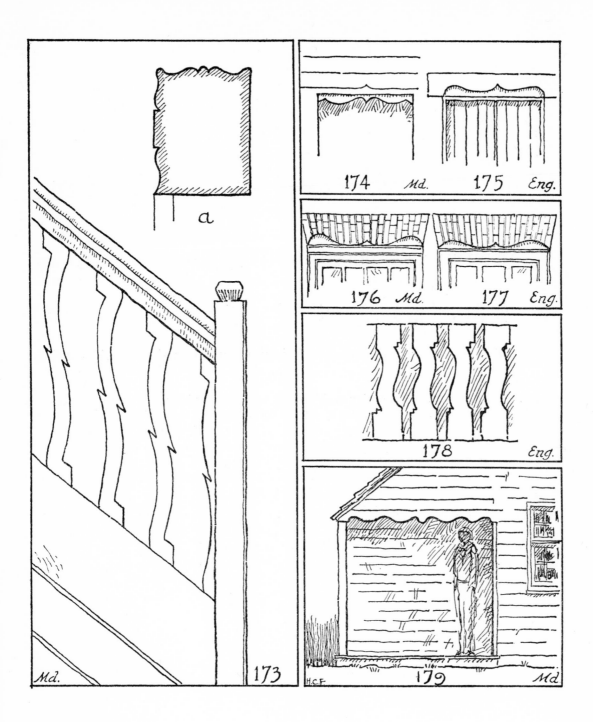

a

174   Md.   175   Eng.

176 Md.   177 Eng.

178   Eng.

Md.   173

H.C.F.   179   Md

MEDIEVAL CROSS-HOUSES IN MARYLAND AND ENGLAND

180. The Brick State House of 1676, St. Mary's City, Maryland. Reconstructed in 1934. Compare with Fig. 181.

181. Brick house between Frosbury and Littlefield Farms, Surrey, England, 1670. (After Davie, 1908)

182. The Court House, Talbot County, Maryland, 1680. A cross-house with a "court hall" at the rear. (Reconstruction drawing by author from specifications in *Maryland Archives*)

180

181

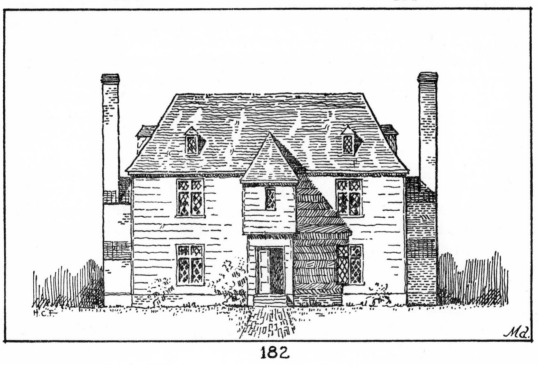

182

V

THE MARYLAND CROSS-DWELLING

THE medieval cruciform house was as popular in Maryland as in Virginia. Like those of the Old Dominion, the Maryland examples were merely buildings of either the hall-and-parlor or the central-passage category, with a porch added to the front and a stair tower, or other kind of wing, at the rear. It is unfortunate that three seventeenth-century examples, of the four known in the Free State, have been destroyed.[1]

The Brick State House of 1676 in St. Mary's City, now reconstructed as a Maryland Tercentenary memorial, was probably the most imposing of the cruciform specimens (Figs. 160, 180).[2] Until its destruction in 1829, it stood, a venerable pile, overlooking the St. Mary's River. In appearance it was a full two stories all around, with a porch and a porch chamber on the front, and a stair tower at the rear. The spacious vestibule on the river bluff had three brick arches, like those at Malvern Hill in Virginia (Fig. 110), and the stair tower possessed a "private door to open into the Garden." The wrought-iron casements with rectangular panes were supported by mullions and transom bars. The summer beams were sixteen-by-twelves (Fig. 147). Medieval pantiles covered the roof; the front and rear wings appear to have had "pyramids" or hip roofs.[3]

As has been heretofore noted, the porch and porch chamber were common features in the old English landscape. One finds them, for instance, at Compton Wynyates, Warwickshire,[4] built in 1520, and at Little Warley Hall, Essex, of the same vintage. On the road between Frosbury and Littlefield Farms in Surrey, England, there stands a brick house (Fig. 181) of 1670 which is in appearance much like the Brick State House of 1676. At Rodd Court, Herefordshire, is another brick porch and porch chamber of the year 1629.[5]

A second cross-house in Maryland was the wooden Talbot County Court House

---

[1] The fourth seventeenth-century cross-house is the well-known old Treasury at Annapolis, built about 1698, and still standing today.

[2] Forman (1938), pp. 285ff.

[3] *Maryland Archives*, II, 404–406.

[4] Tipping, period II, v. 1, p. 119.   [5] *Herefordshire*, III, pl. 164.

on the Eastern Shore (Fig. 182). The order for its erection was enacted in 1679, but it was not actually constructed until 1680–81. In size it was about the same area as the Brick State House at St. Mary's; however, the rear wing was not a stair tower, but a court "hall." In some respects the structure was stylistically in advance of its time, because it had an "Italian" or "hip't" roof, with hipped dormers. The windows were leaded casements, and there were "two stacks of brick chimneys," rising from four fireplaces large enough to take eight-foot logs. The stairway, too, was perhaps slightly in advance of its date, for it is described as being a fair "open well" stair — that is, one passing in straight flights around a square room. Such a stairway was instituted in England about 1600, and was criticized as a waster of space because it left an open well in the center of the stairs.[6]

Be that as it may, the most interesting of the cross-houses of Maryland was Bond Castle (Figs. 183, 185), erected some time in the late seventeenth century upon the Chesapeake Bay shore of Calvert County.[7] Most unfortunately, it was torn down a few years ago to make room for an ugly farm structure. Such became the fate of the most significant rural edifice of Maryland. A first glimpse of Bond Castle from the Bay showed a timber-framed dwelling with steeply-pointed gables and two tall chimneys with inset arches. The main part of the house was only story-and-loft, but the front and rear porches were two full stories high. At each gable of the main part wings, added at a later time, balanced the composition; one a kitchen, the other a bedroom. The external appearance of the old pile was particularly striking because of the overhangs or "jetties" of the front porch chamber, the rear porch chamber, and the peaked gables above them. In truth, at Bond Castle was the only know example of an overhang among the cross-houses of the Old South.

The jetty, or overhanging floor, seems to have been introduced into England from Europe in the fifteenth century. Its origin is due to the medieval method of laying the joists flat, thereby causing a shaky or "dancing" floor; such rickety floors were stabilized by the formation of the jetty, where the weight of the overhanging wall rested on the projecting joists, in the manner shown.

The most important feature of Bond Castle was the front porch, which was decorated with *turned wooden spindles* (Fig. 185a) set in the enclosing wall, and with a curvilinear head on the entrance doorway (Fig. 174). Nowhere else in America is there known to have been a seventeenth-century enclosed vestibule with spindles.

[6] Braun (1940), p. 93.   [7] Forman (1934), pp. 57, 62, 63.

OLD BOND CASTLE IN MARYLAND

183. Bond Castle, Calvert County, Maryland, late seventeenth century. A medieval cross-house with front vestibule having turned spindles — only known example in the United States. (Reconstruction drawing)

184. Parsonage Farm, Much Cowarne, Herefordshire, England, c. 1600, showing an English porch with turned spindles or balusters. (After *Herefordshire*, II)

185. Bond Castle, Calvert County, Maryland, late seventeenth century. Block floor plan. *a*, Detail of turned spindles. *b*, Rear view.

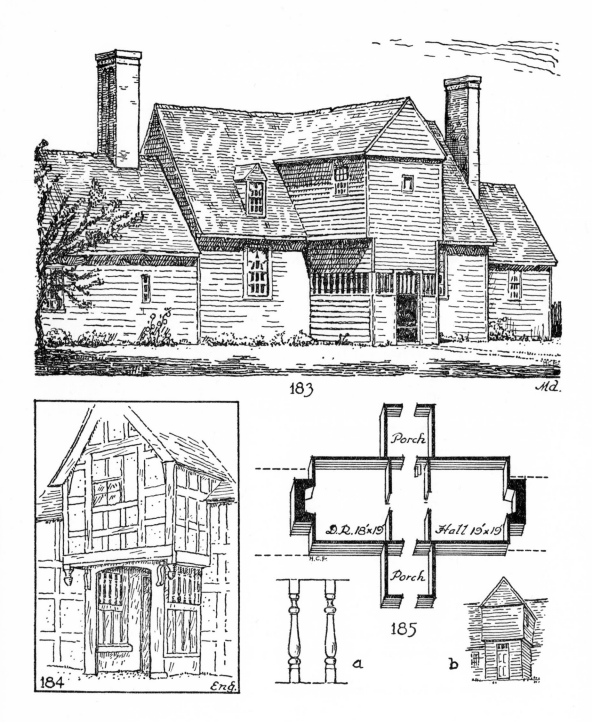

183   Md.

184   Eng.

Porch

D.R. 18'x19'   Hall 19'x19'

H.C.F.

Porch

185

a   b

When Bond Castle was pulled down, a unique architectural monument of medieval style was demolished for all time.

In England the turned spindle was employed in the 1500's, and especially about 1600. There are many existing examples, among which are Hope Farm [8] of the sixteenth century, in Edvin Loach, Herefordshire, where the two-story porch has thick, turned balusters, and also benches on which to sit; Parsonage Farm (Fig. 184), at Much Cowarne, in the same shire, dating from about 1600; and a house at Bourton-on-the-Water, Gloucestershire, where the porch spindles are stone.[9]

The origin of the vestibule with spindles and seats, as exemplified by Bond Castle and the English examples listed above, is undoubtedly derived from the parish church of England. Most of these churches have small side vestibules with benches and traceried windows. It was an obvious step from the wooden mullions of the fifteenth-century Aconbury Church porch, for instance, to the finished, turned balusters of the seventeenth-century church porch of Holy Trinity, Bradwell, Essex.[10] The baluster which looks like a slat on the late fourteenth-century vestibule at Lower Marston manorhouse, Pencombe, Herefordshire, may well form the transitional or intermediary step between Gothic mullion and Jacobean baluster or spindle.

The curvilinear head of the doorway in the entrance porch of Bond Castle was also a Jacobean or Flemish [11] feature. As may be noted from the detail drawing (Fig. 174), the curve was an ogee in the form of a cupid's bow. A coeval English example (Fig. 175) is the curve on the north porch door head of sixteenth-century Pitchford Hall, Shropshire.

The interior of Bond Castle was almost as interesting as the exterior. The house was entered from the front porch by means of a battened door. A nine-foot-wide passageway connected the entrance vestibule with the back porch, and at the rear of this passage stood a tiny winding staircase leading up to the attic bedrooms. Dining room and great hall flanked the passage on either side, each being about nineteen feet square — the dining room perhaps a foot shorter. Both rooms had open beam ceilings. The dining room (Fig. 186) had a chimney ten feet square, and the great fireplace was capacious enough to hold a seven-foot timber. The mantelpiece had Gothic moldings, and the overmantel mural paintings. The central panel was painted to represent, it is supposed, the English home of the Bond family, and the flanking panels showed flower vases. On each side of the fireplace were battened doors with small latches and strap hinges.

How eloquently Bond Castle spoke of a deep-rooted medievalism in America!

[8] *Herefordshire*, II, pl. 31.
[9] Broadbent, pl. 6.
[10] *Herefordshire*, I, pl. 80; III, pl. 42, 108; *Essex*, III, 7.
[11] I.e., Flemish by way of England.

186. THE DINING ROOM OF BOND CASTLE

The mantelpiece had Gothic moldings and the overmantel mural paintings.

(After a water color by Mrs. A. L. Sioussat)

187. TRINITY CHURCH, DORCHESTER COUNTY, MARYLAND, C. 1680
Noted for its Gothic lancet windows, brick buttresses, round apse, and millers' gravestones.

VI

CROSSROADS CHURCHES AND MEETINGHOUSES

THE earliest church erected by Marylanders must have been as Gothic in style as the Old Brick Church, called St. Luke's, in Virginia. The excavations of 1938 in St. Mary's City, Maryland, proved that the brick St. Mary's Chapel — the first Roman Catholic church built by Englishmen in the New World — was in the form of a Latin cross, measuring fifty-seven by fifty-five feet in size (Figs. 194, 195).[1] Its date of erection lay sometime between the founding of that settlement in 1634 and the year 1638, when it was noted, strangely enough, as having been used for Protestant services. During the excavations of 1938 a mullion brick was discovered in the ruins. This kind of brick was employed to separate one casement from another, and therefore, it seems established that the chapel had casement windows. Unfortunately nothing more has been discovered to throw further light on its original appearance.

St. Mary's Chapel was a crossroads church, since it lay at the intersection of St. Mary's Road and Mattapany Street, the oldest thoroughfare in the province.

It is believed that the cross-plan church type came to England from the Continent with the Benedictine monks in the tenth century. The Saxons sometimes employed it, as exemplified by the church at Worth, Sussex.[2] But there is a scarcity of aisleless cross-plans among English parish churches, a fact which makes the Maryland chapel indeed unique. Even so, we are able to compare (Fig. 196) a plan of the late thirteenth-century Church of St. Lawrence, Bishopstone, Herefordshire, with the Chapel of St. Mary's.

There are very few seventeenth-century churches still extant in Maryland — perhaps two at the most. Old Trinity (Fig. 187) in Dorchester appears to have been built as early as 1680, on a cross-plan, with apse, somewhat in the manner of the "Ace of Clubs" Church (Fig. 107) on the Eastern Shore of Virginia. Trinity is now T-shaped, having buttresses on one side of the nave and pointed-arched windows. In addition, the millers' gravestones in front of the church are very interesting to visitors.

---

[1] Forman (1938), pp. 249–251.
[2] Prior (1900), p. 51; Brown (1926–37), p. 237.

MEDIEVAL WAINSCOTING IN MARYLAND AND ENGLAND

188. The Ending of Controversie, Talbot County, Maryland, c. 1670. The master bedroom, and detail of mantel molding.

189. The Ending of Controversie, Talbot County, Maryland, c. 1670. The exterior "palisade" wall, and detail of construction. Compare with Fig. 168.

190. The Ending of Controversie, Talbot County, Maryland, c. 1670. Hall partition, and molding detail.

191. Haddon Hall, Derbyshire, England, fifteenth century, Wainscot screens or partition. Compare with Fig. 190. (After Lloyd, 1931)

192. Old Bloomfield, Talbot County, Maryland, late seventeenth century. Door to attic staircase, and molding detail. (After Forman, 1934)

193. Abbot's Hospital, Guildford, England. Door, and molding detail. Compare with Fig. 192. (After Davie, 1908)

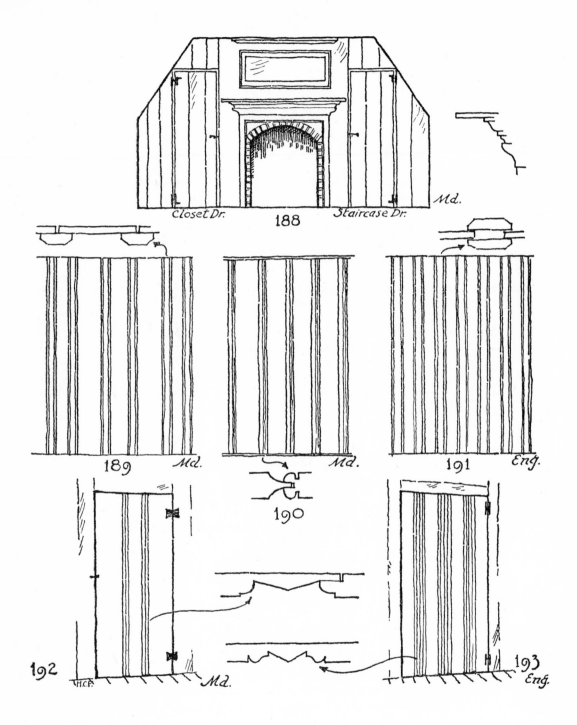

Closet Dr.   188   Staircase Dr.   Md.

189   Md.

190

191   Eng.

192   H.C.P.   Md.   193   Eng.

CROSSROADS CHURCHES AND MEETINGHOUSES OF MARYLAND

194. The Chapel of St. Mary's, St. Mary's City, Maryland, built between 1634 and 1638. First Roman Catholic church erected by the English in the New World. Foundation plan. Length 55 feet, width 57 feet.

195. The Chapel of St. Mary's, St. Mary's City, Maryland. (Approximate reconstruction by the author after excavations)

196. Parish Church of St. Lawrence, Bishopstone, Herefordshire, England, twelfth-fourteenth century. Length, c. 82 feet. (After *Herefordshire*, III, 17)

197. Third Haven Friends' Meetinghouse, Easton, Talbot County, Maryland, 1682. Medieval post-and-beam construction. (Interior, after photograph by author)

198. Third Haven Friends' Meetinghouse, Easton, Talbot County, Maryland, 1682. Cross section, illustrating *x*, addition of 1797; and *y*, guest bedroom used in early times. (After measured drawings by author)

199. Rich Neck Manor, Talbot County, Maryland. The so-called Chapel, soon after 1649 (?). Gothic quatrefoil and ogee arches. Barrel vault shown dotted. Length of structure, 22 feet; width, 12 feet. (Adapted from field notes by author and a photograph in *Gardens of Colony and State*, II)

200. Old Gunpowder Friends' Meetinghouse, Baltimore County, Maryland, 1773. Interior, showing post-and-beam construction in medieval style. Note chamfers and lamb's tongues on posts.

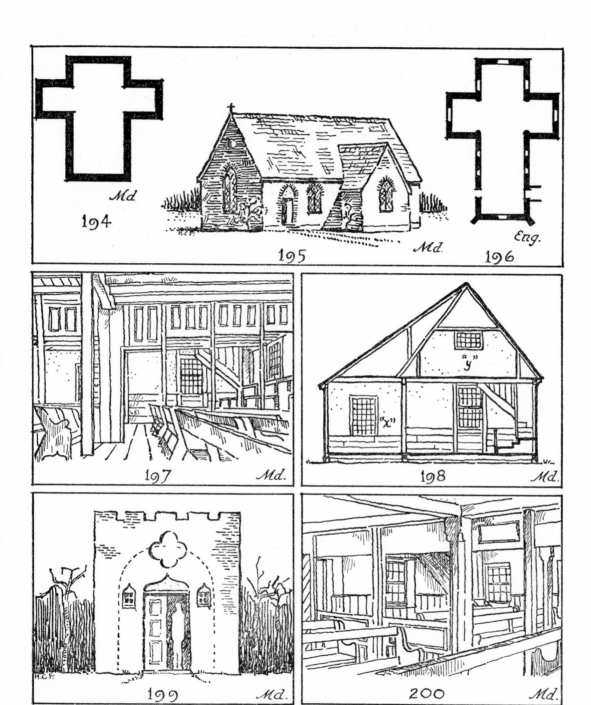

Md.

194

195

Md.

Eng.

196

197   Md.

198   Md.

199   Md.

200   Md.

The Society of Friends commenced religious worship in Maryland as early as 1656, and, consequently, it was not long before crossroads meetinghouses were built. The oldest is Third Haven, at Easton in Talbot County, a frame house of worship erected in 1682 (Figs. 197, 198). It is claimed to be the most ancient church built of wood in the United States. It is likewise noted as the place where William Penn and Lord and Lady Baltimore once attended services. The original size of Third Haven was sixty and a half feet by twenty-two and a half, but in 1797 the width was increased by twelve feet, causing asymmetrical gables. In one corner of the meetinghouse a boxed staircase winds its way to a spacious loft, where guests occasionally were lodged. The main room of worship has a beamed ceiling and exposed post construction in the medieval manner. Four of the original sash windows are in place, seeming to prove that sash was employed as early as 1682 in the province of Maryland.

VII

THE PERSISTENCE OF THE MEDIEVAL STYLE INTO THE NINETEENTH CENTURY

ALTHOUGH the medieval period in the architecture of Maryland terminated, to all intents and purposes, about the year 1700, the great number of later buildings in this style proves that men did not lightly turn to the classical Georgian. The Gothic became deeply intrenched in this colony during the seventeenth century, and no amount of newfangled Georgian mansions, built after the turn of the century in Annapolis, the second capital, could shake the traditional manner of construction.

In the first quarter of the eighteenth century there were three architectural styles current in Maryland, as there were in Virginia. First, the medieval style, with perhaps a detail here or there of classical design; second, the transitional, or halfway stage, between Gothic and Renaissance — a manner which appears to have sprouted in Maryland in the 1670's and 1680's; and last, the classical Georgian, which, in spite of its early characteristics cropping out in the aforementioned transitional style, actually made very slow headway until the 1720's. In the third decade of the eighteenth century there were only a few Georgian houses in the province, such as Harmony Hall, built in 1722–23 in Prince George's County, and Ivy Hall, of 1720, in Somerset County.

The usually accepted line of demarcation between medieval and Georgian periods is, as in Virginia, the introduction of the sash or "guillotine" window. In Maryland the sash seems to have commenced earlier than in Virginia. Several of the great sashes of the Third Haven Meetinghouse, as has already been noted, are still in place, and these probably date from 1682. Walnut Grove (Fig. 211), of 1683, in Queen Anne's County, appears to have retained some of its original sash.

That the sash was employed in the Free State side by side with the casement window in the early eighteenth century may be affirmed from the following comparative references:[1]

---

[1] Tilghman (1915), II, 210.

Casement	*Sash*
1711. Leaded glass windows specified for the Court House of 1711, located near Pitt's Bridge, Talbot County. The lower lights in the windows with transoms were to have had shutters.	1709. Sash windows specified for the Court House, Oxford, Talbot County; followed by a cancellation of the order in favor of "wooden shutters" for the lower part of the windows and "glass" for the upper (evidently a fixed sash).

Consequently it will be seen that the lag of the casement window reached as late as 1711 in the Free State.

It seems appropriate at this point to mention briefly some examples of the four medieval types of house which have already been described as evolving in the seventeenth century and which infiltrated into the succeeding century, and into the nineteenth as well. The reader will remember that first there was the one-room-and-attic cottage, a type which, in the eighteenth century, is well represented by the original portions of Mulliken's Delight (Fig. 207), Prince George's County, and of Old Bloomfield in Talbot County, both erected about 1700. The latter is noted for its medievally-fashioned door (Fig. 192), formed of match boarding fastened on battens. How close the moldings are to those of an ancient battened door (Fig. 193) at the Abbot's Hospital, Guildford, England! The Vailliant House (Figs. 208, 217) in Talbot is also another example of the one-room-and-loft cot in this period.

The hall-and-parlor dwelling is illustrated in the eighteenth century by Mill's Point in St. Mary's County, Lloyd's Landing Farm (Fig. 213) in Talbot, and Lankford House in Somerset. The central-passage type is shown by the latest portion of Holly Hill [2] (c. 1730) in Anne Arundel County (Figs. 239, 249), Fassit House in Worcester County, and stone Summerfield in Baltimore County. In regard to the fourth development, the cruciform dwelling, there stands an excellent example, in brick, by the name of Cedar Hill, in Calvert County, which at one time was owned by the Gantt family.[3] Like its neighbor, earlier Bond Castle, and Christ's Cross and Foster's Castle in Virginia, the main part of the edifice is one and a half stories high, while the porch and porch chamber comprise two. Inside the porch are the customary seats, which in this house have supports carved with Jacobean scrolls. Tall chimneys and tiny lie-on-your-stomach windows, tucked high up in the gables, lend added medieval flavor.

[2] Forman (1934), p. 103.
[3] *Ibid*, p. 67.

Turning now to the second important classification, the transitional house, we may observe the first signs of its advent several years before 1700. These buildings carried touches foretelling the coming change to the Georgian style. The ideal of the Georgian gentleman in the American colonies of the eighteenth century would be to erect a mansion in the classical manner, that is, two rooms deep and two stories and attic high, with wings to balance. It is only natural to find in Maryland in the transition period evidences of a nostalgia for the growing classical feeling in England. Men were outgrowing medieval huts which were one room in thickness and had cramped lofts. Yet, notwithstanding the changes visible in the transitional dwellings, these homes preserved in their main lines a Gothic appearance.

The general reader may identify the first signs of the transition as follows: the sash window, the "pyramid" or hipped roof, the diagonal or cater-cornered fireplace, the catslide roof, the open-well stairs, and the little "aisle" or "cell" at the back of a dwelling.

Perhaps the earliest building of colonial Maryland illustrating transitional tendencies was the Governor's Castle, or St. Peter's (Fig. 148), dating from 1639, in St. Mary's City, which has been previously described, with its great "pyramid" roof surmounted by a cupola. In the Free State there are many transitional types, and we have space to describe only a few.

The first kind of dwelling illustrating the transition is the story-and-loft cottage with a "cell" or "aisle" added to the back of the house in order to give the family bedroom space on the first floor. In most cases the addition of these cells threw the gable roof off center, thereby causing what is known in England as the "catslide" roof (Fig. 130), where one side of the roof is extended almost all the way to the ground. New Englanders call the cell a "lean-to" and the house itself a "salt box." In Maryland there are some very quaint specimens, such as White Hall, built in the late seventeenth century in Talbot County, and the Graeme House, erected in 1743, in Calvert County.

The earliest of these, White Hall (Fig. 201), has one gable end of brick, laid in the English bond. The great hall, only seventeen feet by twenty-three, contains a little winding staircase opposite the fireplace, and a crude box cornice extending along one side of the wall only. At the rear of the dwelling, and just off the hall, are two cells, one a bedroom — a tiny square of about nine feet, with sloping ceiling; the other a dining room with an embryonic, miniature, cater-cornered fireplace, barely able to hold a two-foot log. At White Hall, so low does the catslide roof reach toward the ground that the back door is only five feet and two inches high. Originally the kitchen was a separate building, and it still preserves its ladder to the loft. Walnut Grove

THE TRANSITION IN MARYLAND ARCHITECTURE

201. White Hall, Talbot County, Maryland, late seventeenth century. View, and block floor plan. Note tiny back door.

202. House adjoining the Abbey at Battle, England. (After Hunter, 1930)

203. Carthagena, or Hatton's Corbett, St. Mary's County, Maryland, c. 1711, now destroyed. An example of the central-hall type, with "cells." (After Forman, 1934)

204. Ash Manor Farm, Surrey, England. (After Davie, 1908)

205. Birmingham Manor, Anne Arundel County, Maryland, 1690, now destroyed. The dwelling keeps the medieval porch and overhang, but strives for a formal, balanced effect. (After Sioussat, 1913, and Forman, 1934)

206. John's Point, Dorchester County, Maryland, c. 1665 (?), now demolished. A transitional dwelling with cater-cornered fireplaces and roof jerkins.

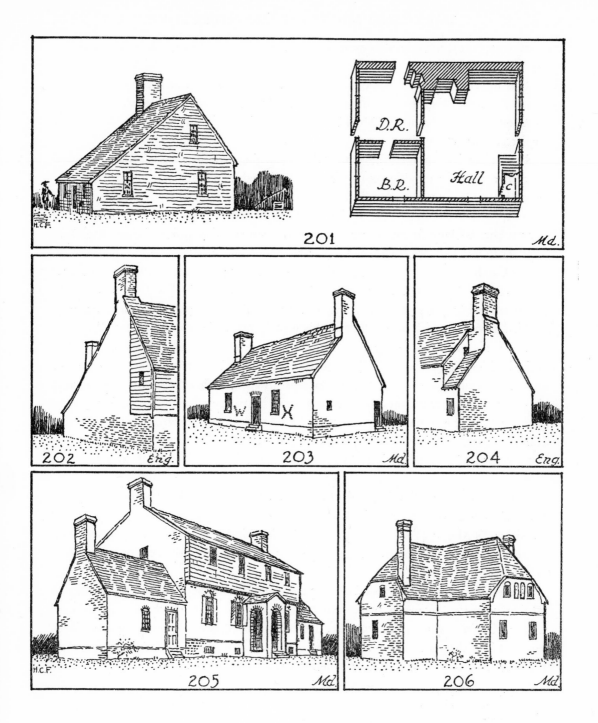

201   D.R.   B.R.   Hall   C   Md.

202   Eng.

203   Md.

204   Eng.

205   Md.

206   Md.

(Figs. 211, 214), a Wright homestead of about 1683, in Queen Anne's County, is much like White Hall.

It is interesting to note that the cater-cornered fireplace seems to have been employed in certain English dwellings from about 1600 onwards. An early example is Wharton Court, Leominster Out, Herefordshire, dating from 1604, with a diagonal fireplace in each corner.[4]

It was not long before the planter, still keeping his little back cells, dispensed altogether with the catslide roof by building his gable symmetrically. He also continued his central passage straight through the cell addition. Thus we come to Carthagena, West St. Mary's, St. Richard's Manor, and Sandgates, all in St. Mary's County and all built in the early eighteenth century; Obligation Farm (1747) in Anne Arundel; and Mt. Eagle (1796) in Charles County. Of these the quaintest by far was Carthagena (c. 1711), totally demolished in 1934 to make a wall for a building in St. Mary's City (Figs. 203, 204, 215).[5] Three sides of the dwelling were brick, the fourth being timber-framed. The naively asymmetrical gable of Carthagena resembled an old English one at Battle Abbey (Fig. 202). Singular, too, was the front façade of this Maryland cottage, for in the brickwork were the glazed initials, "W H" of the builder, William Hebb. This gentleman, it may be noted, was a companion of Lawrence Washington in the Carthagena expedition, and when he returned, he named his dwelling after the fight. In England, brick initials, and even dates, were set in brick walls, as for instance, "1641 W F M," at Hellens Dovecote, Much Marcle, Herefordshire.[6] A narrow passageway crossed the middle of Carthagena, with a boxed staircase in an "ell." The two fireplaces in the cells were small cater-cornered ones.

The old West St. Mary's house (Fig. 216) was very similar to Carthagena, but its brick gable ends were decorated with chimney pents or ingle recesses. At Sandgates, St. Richard's Manor (Figs. 220, 230), and Obligation Farm there is a slight variation of the Carthagena floor plan: the central passage is confined to the rear or cell portion of the dwelling.

Sometimes one comes across a cell type of homestead where there is no passage at all, but only two rooms in front, and two cells in the rear. Such is St. John's, in Charles County, where the staircase, lacking a passageway, appears to have been punched into the wall of the hall (Figs. 218, 224). Access from the dining room to the kitchen-curtain wing was had through an arched doorway in the chimney.

[4] *Herefordshire*, III, 128.
[5] Forman (1934), p. 46.
[6] *Herefordshire*, II, pl. 36.

Still another variety of the transitional, cell class of structure is the cottage with passage running along one gable end. A noteworthy example was Saint Barbara's (Figs. 219, 229), sometimes known as the Troughton-Brome plantation house, in St. Mary's City. Possibly it dated from about 1700, or a little later.[7] There was a huge ingle recess with a sloping brick roof. Inside, a little winding stair led to a dormerless attic containing four little sloped-ceiling bedrooms, each lit by a single pigmy lie-on-your-stomach window. Houses similar in floor arrangement to Saint Barbara's are Turkey Neck in St. Mary's County,[8] The Retreat and Cherry Grove in Charles County, and Brooke Place Manor in Calvert.[9] Of these, The Retreat (Fig. 221), endowed with a picturesque ingle recess, is noted as the home of Daniel of St. Thomas Jenifer, a man who helped to frame the Constitution of the United States.

At the same time, all the transitional houses in Maryland were not marked by cells at the rear. When the planter felt that he could afford it, he not only expanded his cottage in depth, as we have seen, but also on occasion increased it vertically. Consequently a second important transitional type is the narrow, two-story homestead of eighteenth-century vintage, as exemplified by the original Green Park, erected about 1700 in Charles County, or by the much later Thelbert Freeland's House (Figs. 231, 232, 234), of 1786, in Calvert. The gable ends of such piles give evidence of Gothic verticality. Brick Genezir in Worcester County, with its medieval "chevron" brick patterns, is another good specimen of this type.

Sometimes the early Marylander enlarged his house by effacing the pointed, medieval gable and incorporating a roomier gambrel, which is a roof of two slopes on two sides. The gambrel appears to have been employed in the Free State as early as 1683, in Larkin's Hills in Anne Arundel County. This dwelling, sometimes abbreviated to Lark's Hills, was named for its first owner, John Larkin, and is believed to be the same house in which Charles Calvert, Lord Baltimore, and his Council met in 1683. The tall chimneys, the segmental arches with black and red headers over the windows, and the all-header and English bonded brickwork bespeak its early date. Other gambrels in Maryland appear in brick Mulberry Hill, or Malvern Hill (Figs. 235, 238), of 1700, in Anne Arundel County; the wooden Three Sisters, dating from about 1685–90, in Prince George's; Northampton (1704), Lord Fairfax's home in the same county; the original Rose Croft, built about 1706 in St. Mary's City.

By the third decade of the eighteenth century the gambrel became widespread, and we find examples like the Paul Jones House (1733) in Wicomico County; Pemberton

[7] Forman (1938), pp. 240–242.
[8] Forman (1934), p. 41.
[9] *Ibid*, p. 59.

THE PERSISTENCE OF THE MEDIEVAL STYLE IN
EIGHTEENTH-CENTURY MARYLAND

207. Mulliken's Delight, Prince George's County, Maryland, c. 1700. Original portion.

208. Vaillant or Leonard House, Talbot County, Maryland, early eighteenth century. Compare with Fig. 217.

209. Boston Cliff, Talbot County, Maryland, 1792, showing an asymmetrical gable, built purposely off-center. (After Forman, 1934)

210. Fassit House, Worcester County, Maryland, eighteenth century. Compare with Fig. 212. (After Forman, 1934)

211. Walnut Grove, Queen Anne's County, Maryland, c. 1683–1700. An early transitional example, with "catslide" roof. (After Forman, 1934)

212. Fassit House, Worcester County, Maryland, early eighteenth century. Block plan, showing ell in hallway for stairs. (After Forman, 1934)

213. Lloyd's Landing Farm, Talbot County, Maryland, eighteenth century. A hall-and-parlor dwelling. (After Forman, 1934)

214. Graeme House, or Patuxent Farm, Calvert County, 1743. A late transitional example. (After Forman, 1934)

215. Carthagena, St. Mary's County, Maryland, c. 1711, now destroyed. Compare with Figs. 203, 204. (After Forman, 1934)

216. West St. Mary's, St. Mary's County, Maryland, eighteenth century. (After Worthington, 1918)

217. Vaillant House, Talbot County, Maryland, early eighteenth century. An example of the one-room type. Compare with Fig. 208.

218. St. John's, Charles County, Maryland, early eighteenth century. Block plan illustrating hall-and-parlor house with "cells."

219. St. Barbara's, or Troughton-Brome dwelling, St. Mary's City, early eighteenth century, now destroyed. (After Forman, 1938)

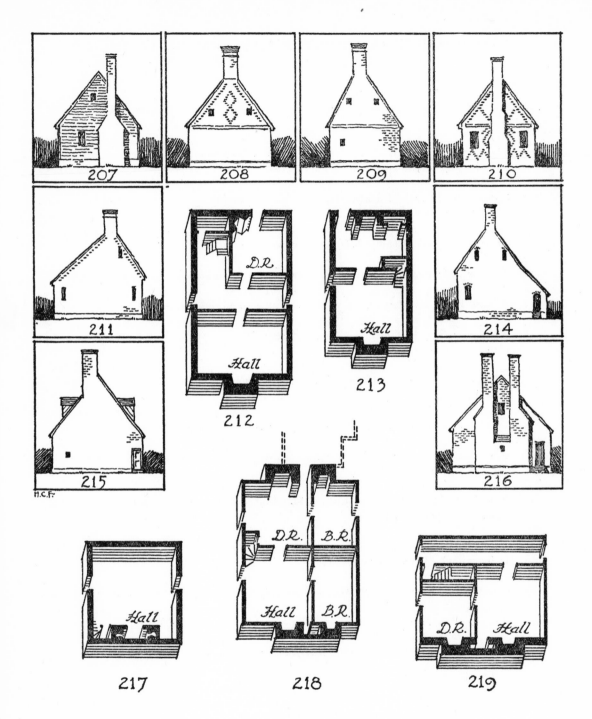

207 208 209 210
211 212 213 214
215 216
217 218 219

H.C.F.

MORE MEDIEVAL DWELLINGS IN EIGHTEENTH- AND NINETEENTH-CENTURY MARYLAND

220. Sandgates, St. Mary's County, Maryland, early eighteenth century. A frame house with brick gables.

221. The Retreat, Charles County, Maryland, probably mid-eighteenth century. A transitional example, with curtain-kitchen wing shown. (After photographs by Mrs. A. L. Ferguson)

222. Mansion Hall, Charles County, Maryland, late seventeenth century. "Cells" added at rear in eighteenth century.

223. Greenwood, Charles County, Maryland, eighteenth century.

224. St. John's, Charles County, Maryland, early eighteenth century. Compare with Fig. 218.

225. Windsor Forest, St. Mary's County, Maryland, late eighteenth century.

226. House near Slyfield Green, Guildford, Surrey, England, probably seventeenth century. (After Davie, 1908)

227. Williams Point, Somerset County, Maryland, probably early eighteenth century, showing black diapering.

228. The Mistake, Charles County, Maryland, probably late eighteenth century.

229. St. Barbara's, or Troughton-Brome House, St. Mary's City, Maryland, early eighteenth century. (After Forman, 1938)

230. St. Richard's Manor, St. Mary's County, Maryland, early eighteenth century. Another transitional type. (Forman, 1934)

231. Clover Fields, Queen Anne's County, Maryland, about 1730. Note use of square stacks in Tudor manner. (After Forman, 1934)

232. Federal Grove, Charles County, Maryland, early nineteenth century. Compare with Fig. 233.

233. House at Wormington, Worcestershire, England. (After Ingemann, 1938)

234. Thelbert Freeland's House, Calvert, Maryland, 1786.

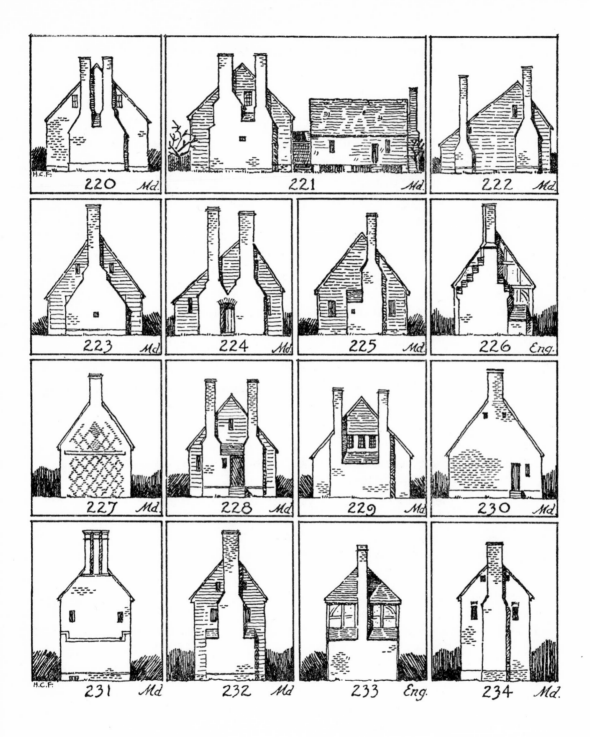

220   Md.

221   Md.

222   Md.

223   Md.

224   Md.

225   Md.

226   Eng.

227   Md.

228   Md.

229   Md.

230   Md.

231   Md.

232   Md.

233   Eng.

234   Md.

Hall (1741) in the same place; Lamb's Meadows (1733) in Kent; or Want Water in Prince George's County. The so-called oldest brick dwelling in Maryland, called Cross Manor, or the Manor of Cornwaleys' Crosse,[10] has been claimed to have been erected in 1642. A bronze marker at the site proclaims this theory. Nevertheless, the use of a gambrel indicates a date later than 1680; and, besides, the floor plan is of a transitional type where the passage runs along the gable end. Cross Manor was probably erected in the early eighteenth century.

Now there are certain unique transitional houses in Maryland which cannot be classified according to type. The first of these was brick John's Point (Fig. 206),[11] believed to have been constructed soon after 1665 — although this date is architecturally too early — on Tobacco Stick Creek in Dorchester County. Its T-shaped plan, steep roof with jerkins,[12] lozenge or black diapered brick patterns, segmental-arched windows and blind windows as well, gave the house a medieval flavor. In their wide bands of polished boards in the forms of a cross, the ceilings of John's Point suggested echoes of medieval summer beams. On the other hand, the broad stairway with walnut hand rail, the hipped roof, the cater-cornered fireplaces, and the curious oblong sash windows, wider than they were tall, indicated the transitional stage.

Another extraordinary specimen of the transition is Bachelor's Hope, said to have been Lord Baltimore's old hunting lodge, and located in the great forests of St. Mary's County.[13] The lodge is an early example of the formal plan: a two-story central portion with flanking, low one-story wings. In the inset front porch are thick round columns of brick and a little "stepladder" winding staircase giving access to the second floor. Some think that the structure harks back to 1679, but the early eighteenth century is the more probable date.

All in all, the known structure which perhaps most graphically represents the transition in Maryland was Birmingham Manor (Fig. 205), erected in 1690 by Richard Snowden, Junior, in Anne Arundel County. The manor was destroyed by fire in 1891. There may be an inclination to doubt a date as early as 1690 for such a large and gracious mansion; nonetheless in this case architectural style agrees with the recorded time of erection. In the first place the mansion was ninety feet long, two stories and attic high in the middle, with one-story wings to balance. At first glance its medieval aspects could be noted: a round-arched enclosed vestibule; the first story of brick, and the second timber-framed — like the Henricopolis buildings of 1611 on the James River; a jetty or overhang of the second story; and segmental

---

[10] Forman (1938), p. 311.
[11] Forman (1934), p. 166.

[12] Small hips near the ridge.
[13] Forman (1934), p. 38.

arches over the windows. But these external trappings failed to reveal the interior floor arrangement. According to reliable accounts, the central passage rose two full stories to the ceiling, in the manner of the baronial halls of England. At the top of the ample stairway, which commenced near the front door, was an open balcony that crossed the spacious hallway in the middle. At the rear were "cells" or "aisles" which in this mansion had developed to a width of twelve feet at the narrowest. The cell fireplaces were cater-cornered. Upon the whole pile lay an exact symmetry, room balancing room and wing equalizing wing.

In the religious architecture of the Free State there is a good eighteenth-century specimen of medieval style: Old Gunpowder Friends' Meetinghouse, erected of stone in 1773 in Baltimore County. There are two great rooms with posts and ceiling beams, battened doors, and a little winding staircase (Fig. 200). These medieval motifs were executed just before the American Revolution.

Even in the great Georgian mansions and their dependencies, medieval characteristics kept cropping up. Chimneys with "withes," those vertical brick projections on the stacks, are found at Caulk's Field (1743), Springfield (1770), and other Kent County dwellings. The medieval black diapering continues in the eighteenth century on Sweet Air (c. 1774) in Baltimore County, and in Fassit House and Genezir in Worcester County (Figs. 85, 210, 227). At Ivy Hall (c. 1720) in Somerset County there are segmental arches. And so the long list of "carry-over" characteristics goes. The medieval style in many instances kept a strangle hold on the Georgian architecture of Maryland.

In the nineteenth century the style continued, though with a kind of delayed momentum. In that dilapidated ghost, Snow Hill Manor, of about 1800, located on the outskirts of St. Mary's City, stands a seventeenth-century type which flourished two centuries later. This is not surprising, perhaps, in an area of Maryland known for its conservatism. Others of like nature are the Pirate House, White Birch, Rosedale, and Glen Mary, all in St. Mary's County and all nineteenth century in date. Towards the middle of the century was erected Cottage Farm in Prince George's County, a little cot with a wooden ingle recess between stone chimneys (Figs. 240, 241). The date, 1842, appears authentic.

The Gothic died hard in Maryland, for even a hundred years ago men were building in that ancient style. In Maryland the last afterglow of medievalism occurred in the 1840's and 1850's, and not in the seventeenth century, which was *the* medieval period in Free State architecture. The Gothic Revival style, that spurious growth, was never aware of the existence of the true medieval style at its very doorstep.

VIII

A SUMMARY OF THE MARYLAND STYLE

THE architecture of Maryland in the seventeenth century, a part of the English medieval period in architecture, first rose in St. Mary's City, early capital of this Province. In that locality freedom of religious worship seems to have induced freedom of architectural design. The variety of building types appears to be greater than that in Virginia. Of the first brick houses erected between the founding of St. Mary's City in 1634 and the year 1639, the Governor's Castle was the most important both from the architectural and the historic viewpoints. Not only was this great pile the home of Lord Baltimore and the royal governors, but it was the largest house of the colonies. Its appearance was unusual. It was exactly square, with rooms of equal size in the corners — somewhat in the manner of certain English Jacobean houses of the time. It had lattice casements; and according to descriptions, a balustraded parapet, a kind of cupola or turret, and one chimney in front of the other. In external semblance the Governor's Castle was much like the great Governor's Palace in Williamsburg, built seventy-four years later. In fact it might be stated that the former was the prototype of the latter.

The ordinary country dwelling in Maryland was a manor house or a plantation house. Such manors were not baronial and ostentatious, as in England, but small in size and plain, like the poor farmers' cottages of Britain. In truth, many of the earliest homes of the Free State were almost wondrously insignificant in size: Henry Potter's dwelling, for instance, having been ten feet long. Lord Baltimore himself, after seeing some structures of this kind, called them very mean and little. Many cottages, like Potter's, had wooden Welsh chimneys built up with posts and wattles.

The Maryland medieval house has approximately the same features as those of Virginia and of England. There is the identical type of wall construction, such as palisades, timber-framing, brick, and part-brick-part-frame, or "half-and-half." This last style, the half-and-half dwelling, generally has the gable ends of brick, and wooden sides; but sometimes there is but one brick gable, as in the Leigh House in St. Mary's City, or three walls of brick, as in Carthagena.

The town house in the Free State, in keeping with Lord Baltimore's written instructions, was a row house in the manner of those in Jamestown and London. The row houses so far discovered by the writer stood along the highway in St. Mary's City known as Aldermanbury Street. They may be identified tentatively as "A town house within the Fort," and the Secretary's Office, sometimes called the Council Chamber. Their gable ends faced the street on one side and the St. Mary's River on the other.

The evolution of the medieval country house in this province, like that of Virginia, followed a course from the one-room-and-attic shelter to the great Georgian mansion of the eighteenth century. There are, as first examples, the original portions of the Leigh House in St. Mary's and Holly Hill in Anne Arundel County, representing cottages of but one room and loft. Next came the hall-and-parlor dwelling, and of these there are a fair number in Maryland: Clocker's Fancy, a "half-and-half" house; brick Preston and Resurrection Manor; wooden Mansion Hall; and the "palisaded" lodging known as The Ending of Controversie; and the like. It was a simple matter to block off the great hall of any of these hall-and-parlor homes to make a new type, the central-passage habitation, illustrated by Make Peace and My Lord's Gift.

Of these seventeenth-century examples, two are worthy of especial note: Mansion Hall — a tiny cot in spite of its name — possessing Jacobean pierced splat balusters and a Gothic, molded handrail; and The Ending of Controversie, built about 1670 in the Anglo-Saxon manner of palisades by Wenlocke Christison, a pioneer of religious freedom in this country.

It was an easy matter to form the next stage in the development of the country house by adding a porch on the front and a wing at the rear. In this way began the cross-dwelling in Maryland, of which there are, or were, a few examples, such as the Brick State House of 1676, a two-story edifice now reconstructed in the City of St. Mary's; the wooden Court House of Talbot County, with an "Italian" or hipped roof; and gray Bond Castle, that epitome of medievalism so wantonly destroyed to make elbow room for an unsightly farmhouse. Bond Castle had the only known medieval enclosed vestibule with turn spindles in all the New World. The custom of employing spindles or balusters on the porches of ancient English country houses was doubtless derived from the traceried windows of the parish church vestibules.

The characteristics of Maryland medieval architecture — chiefly the brick architecture — are much the same as in Virginia, with the following exceptions: *no corbie or crow-stepped gables; no chimneys on the long sides of the house; no curvilinear gables; no "diamond" stacks; no fancy pargetry; and no hooded fireplaces.* To our knowledge none of these features has yet been discovered in the Free State. On the other hand, it is reasonable to assume that many edifices of this province at one time possessed these motifs.

MORE MEDIEVAL DWELLINGS IN LATER MARYLAND; CHIMNEYS IN ENGLAND AND MARYLAND

235. Loch Leven, Charles County, Maryland, late eighteenth century. A transitional dwelling with gambrel roof.

236. House in Calvert County, Maryland, eighteenth century. The addition of "cells" made a quaint gable end.

237. Fox's Harbor, St. Mary's County, Maryland, eighteenth century.

238. Mulberry Hill, or Malvern Hill, Anne Arundel County, Maryland, early eighteenth century.

239. Holly Hill, Anne Arundel County, Maryland, showing the later wing, dating c. 1730. Compare with Fig. 249.

240. Mount Pleasant, Anne Arundel County, Maryland, 1830. (HABS)

241. Cottage Farm, Prince George's County, Maryland, 1842.

242. Hatton's Mansion, or Chapel Hill, Prince George's County, Maryland, late eighteenth century. Two-storied ingle recess on a Georgian mansion. (After photograph by Mrs. A. L. Ferguson)

243. House near Lynch, Kent County, Maryland, probably mid-eighteenth century, showing stepped chimney. Compare with Fig. 244.

244. House at Walkern, near Stevenage, Herefordshire, England, illustrating stepped chimney. (After Oliver, 1929)

245. Kentwell Hall, Suffolk, England. Chimney with inset arches. (After Garner and Stratton, I)

246. Wye House, Talbot County, Maryland, c. 1662. Original brick house with chimney stack having "withe."

247. Houses at Petworth, Sussex, England (*left*), and near Newenden, Kent, England (*right*). Compare *left* with Fig. 246. (After Holmes, 1906)

248. Bond Castle, Calvert County, Maryland, late seventeenth century, illustrating chimney with inset arches. Compare with Figs. 183, 245.

Furthermore, in addition to the Maryland characteristics suggested above, others have been discovered which do not appertain to the Virginia list, as for example: *overhanging gables or stories, formerly known as jetties; pierced splat balusters and Gothic molded handrails; ingle recesses or chimney pents with brick roofs; curvilinear heads to doorways; chimneys with withes; and turned spindles in an enclosed vestibule.*

Then there are literary references to other peculiarities of the Middle Ages: *the Welsh or country chimney of wood; the sealed stairs, or staircase; the wicket, or little door within a big door; and the white oak mantel tree.*

About 1700, three architectural styles flourished in Maryland: the medieval, with minor classical details; the transitional or halfway stage; and the classical Georgian, which actually made slow progress until the 1720's. The usual demarcation between medieval and Georgian periods is the introduction of the sash window, which in Maryland seems to have been incorporated as early as 1680. However that may be, casement windows were still being employed in some buildings way past the turn of the century. For instance, there were casements upon the Talbot County Court House of 1711.

The various kinds of medieval country house which flourished in the seventeenth century persisted into the eighteenth. The one-room-and-loft cottage is represented by the original part of Mulliken's Delight, and the Vailliant House; the hall-and-parlor dwelling by Lloyd's Landing Farm and the Lankford House; the habitation with central passage by the Fassit House and the latest section of Holly Hill; and the cruciform-plan by Cedar Hill or the Gantt House.

The first signs of the transition in the Free State are marked by the use of the sash window, the hipped roof, the cater-cornered fireplace, the catslide roof, the open-well stairs, and the little back "cell" or "aisle," added toward the end of the seventeenth century and in the beginning of the eighteenth at the rear of the house to make an extra room for the growing family. One finds domiciles of this kind in White Hall in Talbot County and in Carthagena, Sandgates, and West St. Mary's, in St. Mary's County. Other types of the transition are illustrated by St. John's in Charles County, where the passage is omitted altogether and the tiny staircase appears punched into the wall; Saint Barbara's, where the passage runs along one gable end; the Thelbert Freeland House, with its narrow two-story gables; gambrel-roofed Larkin's Hills and Northampton and Cross Manor; John's Point, with its peculiar windows; Bachelor's Hope, an early example of the formal plan; and last, but not least, Birmingham Manor, a ninety-foot mansion with medieval overhang and cater-cornered fireplaces.

249. HOLLY HILL, ANNE ARUNDEL COUNTY, MARYLAND

An example of medieval architecture (*left*, c. 1667) and of the persistence of medieval style into the eighteenth century (*right*, c. 1730). Note the Jacobean curvilinear window head.

In the nineteenth century the medieval style continued, but more slowly. Such an abode as Cottage Farm of 1842, possessing the old, old style of ingle recess or chimney pent, fills one with astonishment that the medieval style of architecture could have approached so near the threshold of the twentieth century. How close to the edge of medievalism, at least in the realm of architecture, is the modern world!

250. THE ORIGINAL HOLLY HILL (c. 1667)

PART IV
Medieval Architecture of the Deep South

I

BERMUDA

THE history of the architecture of the Bermuda Islands, an English colony, begins almost as soon as that of Virginia. It was only two years after the founding of Jamestown in 1607 that Sir George Somers was shipwrecked on the Bermudas. News of this accident, spreading throughout England, perhaps caused Shakespeare to have the characters in *The Tempest* shipwrecked in the "still-vexed Bermoothes." By 1612, Governor Richard More, accompanied by "men, women and mariners,"[1] made a settlement there and built the customary fort and storehouse.

The earliest structures erected on the islands were medieval cottages and cabins, made of cedar timbers — probably punches set into the ground, as in Virginia — and of palmettoes for the roof. Nevertheless, the first important dwelling, which was constructed in 1612 for the Governor, was made in the old English oak tradition of timber-framing. It is scarcely necessary to remind the reader of the coeval "faire" cottages, two stories and cornloft high, on the James City street of 1611. A second timber-framed edifice was built in Bermuda in 1618 in the form of a cross. The old chronicle tells of it, thus: "the governour framed a pretye hansome house contrived into the fashion of a cross." It is said that the cross shape gave additional strength to this dwelling and buttressed it at times of hurricane. No doubt this cruciform example set the precedent for a whole series of structures fabricated in the Bermudas down to the middle of the eighteenth century.

From the drawing in Captain John Smith's *General History* (1624) it is manifest that Bermudians erected row dwellings with their gables facing the street in the approved London and Jamestown medieval manner. He also pictures the first Bermuda church (Fig. 258) with buttresses, mullioned windows with diamond-pane casements, and a side vestibule. These characteristics are all common to the English parish church of the Middle Ages.

By 1619, Governor Nathaniel Butler, the man who once claimed that Virginians built the meanest houses that he had ever seen, arrived in the Bermudas as governor and erected in the winter of 1620–21 what is believed to have been the first stone building in the Colony. This was the "Town House," or State House at St. George's.

---

[1] Andrews (1934–38), I, 216.

BERMUDA ARCHITECTURE OF MEDIEVAL STYLE

251. Tankfield, Paget, Bermuda, between 1700 and 1720. A cruciform dwelling. Compare with Figs. 160, 254. (After photograph by Dr. Henry Wilkinson)

252. Old House at Harrington Sound, Bermuda, illustrating Jacobean gables and embryonic pediment. Compare with Fig. 253.

253. Old House at Harrington Sound, Bermuda. West gable. Compare chimney and division of flues with those in Fig. 255. (After Humphreys, 1923)

254. Tankfield, Paget, Bermuda, between 1700 and 1720. Block floor plan. (After drawing owned by Dr. Henry Wilkinson)

255. Cottage at Bromfield, Shropshire, England. Compare with Fig. 253. (After Parkinson, 1904)

256. Cottage on the Tankfield place, Paget, Bermuda, early eighteenth century.

257. Tankfield, Paget, Bermuda. Cross section showing tray ceiling.

258. The church at St. George's, Bermuda, 1622. (Redrawn from Smith, *General History*, 1624)

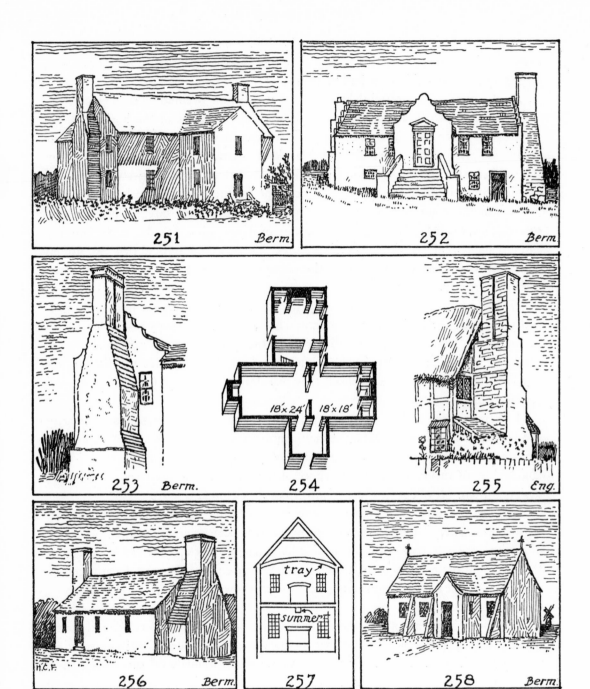

251   Berm.

252   Berm.

253   Berm.

18'x 24' 18'x18'

254

255   Eng.

256   Berm.

tray

summer

257

258   Berm.

Illustrated in Smith's *General History*, the edifice stands today without its upper story. It was built of the native aeolian limestone, and it comprised downstairs a fair, large room of about thirty-six feet by twenty.

By the early 1620's certain characteristics peculiar to Bermuda were evident: the stone-slab roofs which are pitched not over forty-five degrees to the horizontal, because of the hazards of the hurricane; "bottled" chimneys — something like the great "pyramid" chimneys of Virginia and Maryland — employed as quasi buttresses on the southeast side of the dwellings for a support against hurricanes; stucco to cover the limestone blocks, and whitewash and cement for the roof; the enclosed vestibule in front of the house which was a symbol of hospitality; the tall outdoor entrance stairway, known as "welcoming arms" because of its spreading or splay at the bottom; and casement windows with bottle-glass panes. There were also butteries, two-storied outhouses with massive walls to keep the victuals cool; and there were tanks to catch rainwater from the roof.[2]

On the inside of Bermuda houses of the seventeenth century, ceilings were generally beamed, although some were trays. A tray ceiling perhaps resembled an inverted service tray; it was high, filling part of the space under the rafters. For ventilation in hot weather the tray made a surprisingly cool house. Hearths did not project in front of the fireplace; instead, they were raised knee-high from the floor and remained flush with the walls.

In Bermuda the barge or verge board and the projecting eaves are not ordinarily encountered. There are no extant separate chimney stacks or flues as in Virginia and England. But there seem to be a number of Jacobean, or Flemish-by-way-of-England, gables of curvilinear or crow-stepped shape. The quaint gable end of Jacobean design is more prevalent in these islands than in Virginia.

Not many structures of authentic seventeenth-century date can be pointed out in Bermuda. Cluster Cottage, Warwick, seems to have been originally a one-story home of three rooms with tray ceilings built in a long, narrow block.[3] The stone cottage on the Tankfield place (Fig. 256), Paget, represents in general the seventeenth-century small house type; the accompanying illustration shows several of the characteristics already described.

The Bermudian has always been conservative in his building styles, and consequently, it is not surprising to find that the local medieval style strongly persisted in the eighteenth century. One of the best examples of the medieval survivals in Bermuda is Tankfield itself (Figs. 251, 254), a cross-house built between 1700 and 1720

---

[2] Browning MS.   [3] Humphreys (1923), p. 26.

at Paget.[4] It stands on property granted to Lord Paget and possessed later by the Pym family. This fabric, with its enclosel porch and porch chamber and rear wing, bears a striking resemblance to the Brick State House of 1676 at St. Mary's City in Maryland. One of the chimneys of Tankfield is outside, like those of the Maryland edifice, but the other is inbuilt, with closets or small cupboards flanking the fireplace on either side. There is an open beam ceiling, like that of the Maryland building, but upstairs the tray ceiling, peculiar to Bermuda, is employed. The sketch (Fig. 257) of the cross section of Tankfield illustrates these points.

Another Bermuda cruciform structure something like the St. Mary's City State House is the Old Williams Home, Devonshire. It has seen many changes. Once it was a farmhouse, then a golf club; later it became a farm again. Later additions include a spurious veranda and a bathroom "wart" stuck on beside a great chimney. The roof has hips — what were known in the Maryland State House as "pyramids" — and the chimneys are all outside ones. Still another two-story cross-dwelling is Inwood, constructed soon after 1722 at Paget. The former home of Francis Jones, President of the Governor's Council, this estate was considered the best on the islands.

Of the Jacobean examples in Bermuda, one of the most outstanding is the cruciform cottage of one story and cellar at Harrington Sound (Figs. 252, 253).[5] The gables of the vestibule and rear wing are curvilinear, in this case designed with little short curves and unobstructed by chimneys. Incipient or embryonic pediments are employed over the front door and over the gable windows in the wing at the back. How reminiscent they are of the incipient pediments of Bacon's Castle in Virginia, and of buildings such as Ripley Manor in England!

Additional Jacobean gables of curvilinear style are seen at The Chimneys, Paget;[6] a house near Riddle's Bay, Warwick; a dwelling in Sandys Parish; and several homes in St. George. Crow-step gables exist on old houses in Devonshire, Bermuda, and likewise on the north shore of Hamilton Parish.

It may be concluded that the seventeenth century was the medieval period in Bermuda architecture. At this time there developed a strongly traditional English architecture, in many respects closely related to the early buildings of Maryland and Virginia. In the eighteenth century the style of the Middle Ages persisted in such notable examples as Tankfield and Inwood. It was only here and there throughout the islands that Jacobean influence in design did creep in, as may be seen today in the cuspings and steppings on certain whitewashed cottages besides the summer seas.

[4] From data kindly supplied by Dr. Henry Wilkinson, Hamilton, Bermuda.
[5] Humphreys, p. 247, and photographs supplied by Henry Wilkinson.
[6] Humphreys, p. 111.

II

NORTH CAROLINA

THERE are fewer examples of medieval architecture in the two Carolinas, because these colonies were settled many years after the founding of Virginia and Bermuda. Of course, there was once upon a time the impermanent settlement of Roanoke Island in North Carolina, described in a previous chapter. Nevertheless this early village of thatched buildings never belonged to North Carolina, nor is very much known about it.

Except for another small village existing from 1665 to 1667 on the Cape Fear River in North Carolina, which possessed structures about which nothing is known today, the history of the early architecture of this state may be said to have commenced in that region between Virginia and Albemarle Sound. First as explorers and later as homeseekers, Virginians began moving into this region as early as 1653.[1] They lived on small farms and tended livestock, tobacco, and corn. In 1664, William Drummond, that Scotchman who saved the records upon the burning of Jamestown by Bacon, was appointed governor of the province of Albemarle. In this way began the colony of North Carolina.

As might be expected, the early architecture has a distinctly Virginian cast. There are samples of dwellings which are similar in flavor to those of Virginia and Maryland. We find the same one-room-and-loft structures, the same hall-and-parlor habitations, and the identical central-passage types. Most of the North Carolina specimens have been destroyed, but in the eighteenth century we discover several medieval-styled survivals to help round out the picture.

The simplest timber-framed hut is represented by the Little Riddick House (Fig. 259) in Gates County in the Albemarle region.[2] Probably dating from the beginning of the eighteenth century, it possesses one chamber about eighteen feet by twelve; an inside gable-end chimney, now destroyed; a ladder to the loft in one alcove, and a closet with window in the other. A feature of this cottage is the batten door, heavily studded with wrought-iron nails in an over-all diaper pattern. The John Roberts

---

[1] Andrews (1934–38), III, 195.
[2] HABS; Johnston and Waterman (1941), p. 26.

House (Fig. 260) in the same county, built perhaps a few years later, is a more capacious one-room example, with an attic made accessible by a stairway instead of a ladder.

In the early eighteenth century the Thomas White dwelling, near Bethel in Pitt County, illustrates the hall-and-parlor variety; and the White-Newbold House (Fig. 281) in Perquimans County marks the central-passage type. The latter example, it may be noted, resembles the Warburton House (Fig. 52) in Virginia, in being one-and-a-half stories high, all brick, with steep roof and tall inside chimneys. It has also the little arched gable windows like those of the Virginia house. The central passage is only about four feet wide, and, of necessity, the boxed winding stair projects into the "great hall" in exactly the manner of that at Brick Billy in Virginia (Fig. 117). The chimneys, too, are ornamented with chimney caps having a plaster necking, in the fashion of Maryland and Virginia.

Other examples of medieval style flourishing in eighteenth-century North Carolina are the brick Walton House (Fig. 263) in Chowan County, with its great beamed fireplace and open-beamed ceiling; the Gregory House in Camden County, which originally formed a story-and-loft brick cottage with outside chimney; [3] the so-called Old Brick House (Fig. 264) near Elizabeth City, dating after 1750; and wooden Cascine (Fig. 265), near Louisburg, with its little gable window. [4]

As in Maryland and Virginia, the addition of a small back "cell" or "aisle" marked the first transitional stage to the great Georgian mansion. In Perquimans County, the Davis dwelling (Fig. 262), its quaint gables decorated with chevrons in glazed brick, has rooms added to the rear in order to take the overflow of a large family. The Wythe House (Fig. 261), near Raleigh, is in this respect like the Davis House. Further, it was not long before the men of North Carolina went about erecting another kind of transitional habitation, the gambrel-roofed dwelling, such as Wakefield (1760) in Wake County, and Bockover House (1767) in Chowan County. [5]

Throughout the second half of the eighteenth century medieval influence seems to have persisted chiefly in the use of black diapering, and the ingle recess or chimney pent. The Alexander Long House, or Long's Ferry, built in 1783 near Salisbury in Rowan County, has a projecting brick ingle situated between tall chimneys, which are faced with hearts and the initials of the owners in brick glazing (Fig. 86). Large diamonds mark the gable of the two-story Walton House (1755), [6] near Hobbville,

[3] HABS.
[4] EAA.
[5] HABS.
[6] Johnston and Waterman (1941), p. 65.

THE MEDIEVAL STYLE IN NORTH CAROLINA

259. Little Riddick House, vicinity of Gates, Gates County, North Carolina, showing medieval nail-studded door. (After HABS, photograph by Waterman)

260. John Roberts House, Carter Farm, Gates County, North Carolina. (After HABS)

261. Wythe House, near Raleigh, Wake County, N. C. (After EAA, Library of Congress)

262. Davis House, vicinity of New Hope, Perquimans County, North Carolina. An addition was made on the right side of this building. (After HABS)

263. Walton House, Chowan County, near border of Gates County, North Carolina.

264. Old Brick House, vicinity of Elizabeth City, Pasquotank County, North Carolina, soon after 1750. (After photograph in EAA)

265. Cascine, an old Perry house, vicinity of Louisburg, Franklin County, N. C., in use before 1775. (After photograph in EAA)

266. Cupola House, Edenton, Chowan County, North Carolina, probably about 1715. (Detail showing medieval overhang and Jacobean brackets)

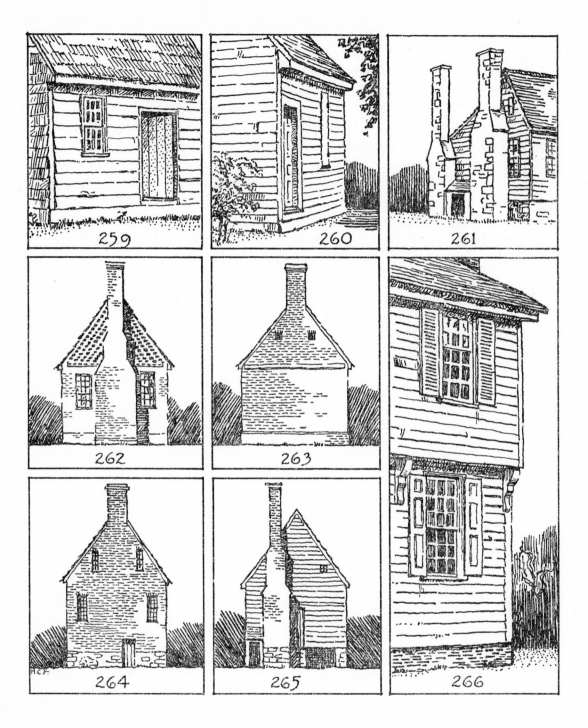

259

260

261

262

263

264

265

266

in Gates County, and Oak Grove (1782) in Gaston County. Even the Stigerwalt House, erected in 1811 in Rowan County, has them.

There seems to be no evidence of the cross-dwelling in North Carolina. Nonetheless, there is a very fine timber-framed dwelling of Jacobean style standing in Edenton. This is the Cupola House (Fig. 266), built probably about 1715. Of course it dates about sixty-five years after Bacon's Castle in Virginia, but its characteristics are nearly as interesting. The second floor has jetties or overhangs with curvilinear hewn brackets. The tall gables have carved finials. The oval window on the front gable is reminiscent of that at Foster's Castle and the tower of the Old Brick Church in Virginia (Figs. 87, 109). The overhanging second story smacks of Bond Castle in Maryland. In the Cupola House, North Carolina has the best example of an existing wooden house in the Jacobean tradition in all America.

III

SOUTH CAROLINA

THE first settlement by Englishmen in South Carolina was established in 1670 by Sir Anthony Ashley Cooper and John Locke at Old Town, or Old Charles Town, located about twenty-five miles from the Atlantic Ocean. Nothing is known about the appearance of the buildings there. In 1680 the present city of Charleston was founded at the junction of the Ashley and Cooper Rivers — a site better adapted for defense and health than the former village. In 1681, there were more than twenty structures in Charleston. In colonial times this city became the most important town south of Philadelphia.[1]

The terms of the Carolina charter from the King reproduced the seignorial privileges of a baronial lord in England, but there is no record of courts baron and courts leet, as in Maryland. The proprietors of South Carolina stood at the top of a feudal pyramid. Each one owned a seignory of twelve thousand acres of land in each county; below them stood the landgraves; and still lower the caciques, the lords of the manors, and the plain yeomen.

Medieval architecture flourished in South Carolina, as it did in the other colonies of the Old South to the northward. Nevertheless, very few examples remain. The oldest house on record in the state, brick Medway (Fig. 267), was constructed in 1686 by Jean d'Arsens, called Seigneur de Weirnhoudt, a man who led a small company of Dutchmen to Carolina. The habitation seems to have had lattice casements [2] in common with the medieval buildings of Maryland and Virginia. Its chief claim to distinction, however, is the crow-stepped gable — in this particular case, of direct Flemish or Dutch derivation. But for any difference in appearance they might have just as well been Flemish-by-way-of-England gables (Fig. 268). The floor plan conforms to the transitional type, since on one side the structure is two rooms deep. In later years various additions were made, but the stepped gables were always faithfully copied. Furthermore, the front and rear façades were of equal importance, a scheme usually employed in this region.

[1] Andrews (1934–38), III, 202.
[2] Stoney (1938), p. 89.

THE MEDIEVAL AND JACOBEAN STYLES IN SOUTH CAROLINA

267. Medway, South Carolina, 1686. Transitional house with crow-step gable. (Restoration, adapted from Stoney, 1938)

268. House near the railway station, Wroxham, Norfolk, England, c. 1610–1630. (After Oliver, 1912)

269. Middleburg, South Carolina, 1699. Exposed post-and-beam construction, vertical board partition, and batten door.

270. Hanover House, Clemson, South Carolina, 1716. Formerly situated on site of Santee-Cooper Reservoir, near Charleston. Note medieval style of T-shaped chimney, and of chimney pent. (After photograph in *Atlanta Journal Magazine*)

271. Mulberry, or Mulberry Castle, South Carolina, 1714. Square floor plan in Jacobean style. Compare Figs. 150, 151, 272.

272. Mulberry, or Mulberry Castle, South Carolina, 1714. Towers with curvilinear roofs in Jacobean style. Transitional gambrel roof with jerkin-headed gables.

273. Middleton Place, South Carolina, 1755. South wing. Curvilinear gables in Jacobean style.

274. Earlham Hall, England. Jacobean home of Elizabeth Fry. (After a photograph from the American Friends Service Committee)

275. North Chacham Stable, South Carolina, c. 1760. Another Carolina gable in Jacobean style. (After Stoney, 1938)

267 S.C.

268 Eng.

269 S.C.

270 S.C.

271 S.C.

272 S.C.

273 S.C.

274 Eng.

275 S.C.

THE PERSISTENCE OF MEDIEVAL STYLE IN NINETEENTH-CENTURY GEORGIA

276. Old House at Gray, Jones County, Georgia, early nineteenth century. Note chimney pent and kitchen connected with house by colonnade.

277. A Negro house, Decatur, Georgia, late nineteenth century. The "outshut," or little rear "cell," is in the style of the Middle Ages.

278. Negro houses, near Randolph Street, Atlanta, Georgia, nineteenth century. Row gables in medieval style.

279. Old house or quarters, 413 East Bryan Street, Savannah, Georgia, early nineteenth century. Here are batten doors, beamed ceilings, vertical board partitions, and winding staircases.

280. Old house near Stone Mountain, DeKalb County, Georgia, early nineteenth century, perhaps 1850. Main house (left) of transitional style, two rooms deep, two wide. Freestanding chimneys. Horizontal board interior paneling. Quarters to right. Porches modern.

276

277

278

279

280

One of the oldest existing wooden dwellings, if not the most ancient in South Carolina, is Middleburg,[3] constructed in 1699, at the end of the seventeenth century. This house is transitional, in that, although conforming to the Gothic thickness of one room, it is two stories in height. The rooms were planned end to end in order to give a maximum of ventilation — so it is said. In contrast to the gable-end chimneys of Medway, Middleburg has central back-to-back fireplaces. The north end of the house and the porches appear to be an addition. Inside, the medieval-style post construction (Fig. 269) is exposed, and vertical boarding forms the wainscot. The doors are battened and carry H–L hinges.

The medieval style of architecture in South Carolina persisted into the eighteenth century in the same way that it did in North Carolina, Virginia, and Maryland. For instance, there is a transitional house by the name of Hanover (Fig. 270), of 1720, which was brought from the site of the Santee-Cooper Reservoir near Charleston to Clemson. This fabric has a gambrel roof, T-shaped chimney stacks and an ingle recess, and is two rooms deep. Old Mulberry, or Mulberry Castle as it is sometimes called (Figs. 271, 272), was erected in 1714 by Thomas Broughton, and conforms to the square type of Jacobean floor plan with corner towers, such as is found at Bolsover Castle in Derbyshire, England, of 1613. While the roof of the middle part of Mulberry is a gambrel with jerkin-headed gables, the tower or pavilion roofs possess Jacobean curves — an unusual example in America. Even Middleton Place (1755), the stable of North Chachan (1760), and St. Stephen's Parish Church (1767) carry Jacobean gable ends (Figs. 273–275) in the manner of Bacon's Castle and the English prototypes.

[3] *Ibid*, p. 47.

281. THE WHITE-NEWBOLD HOUSE, NEAR HERTFORD, PERQUI-
MANS COUNTY, NORTH CAROLINA

Similar to a medieval type of house in Virginia.

282. THE THORNTON HOUSE, GREEN COUNTY, GEORGIA
Illustrating an ingle recess of medieval style in the heart of the Deep South.

IV

GEORGIA

WHILE medieval architecture, per se, did not flourish in Georgia, since the first settlement, Savannah, was not established until 1733, this style of building strongly persisted in the history of the architecture of this state. Yet it is surprising to discover that some of the earliest structures in Georgia were erected in the Anglo-Saxon manner of palisades. As has already been described, this is the method of setting vertical planks or tree trunks side by side into the earth. The fort of Frederico, Georgia, encompassed its buildings with a palisaded wall.[1] At the Bethesda Orphan House, erected in 1739 near Savannah, the Infirmary, the Kitchen House, and the Cart House were also made of palisades. Even Midway Church itself was enclosed by vertical timbers, fourteen feet long, sunk five feet in the earth.[2]

The dwellings of the early settlers of Savannah were generally of two kinds: huts, and timber-framed habitations.[3] The former were probably flimsy puncheoned structures, and like the Virginia cabins of the same category, "worse than nought." The framed cottages were about sixteen feet by twenty-four — the exact dimensions of some of the town houses at Jamestown in Virginia. They had sides of unplaned boards, floors of rough "deal" boards, and roofs of shingle. An old view of Savannah [4] in 1734 shows cottages of what might be called the "William May" type of dwelling, because they look so much like the home of that gentleman in old Jamestown (Fig. 36a). On each cottage a flush or inside chimney rose at one gable end; but the roof was flatter than that of Virginia.

A description of one of these early Georgia contraptions has come down to us. A man by the name of Sir Francis Bathurst, of Bathurst Bluff, lived in a two-room clapboarded domicile, through which the wind howled at will. His quarters measured only twelve feet wide and twenty long, and comprised only a dining room and a sleeping chamber.[5]

[1] Corry (1930), p. 186.
[2] Cooney (1933), p. 4.
[3] Corry, pp. 192, 194.

[4] Anderson (1933), pl. 1.
[5] Corry (1930), p. 197.

Perhaps the quaintest medieval survival in Georgia is the Thornton House (Fig. 282), erected about 1780, in Green County; yet except for its ingle recess or chimney pent of Gothic flavor, this dwelling could be labeled a good example of the English Georgian style in America. The doorway in the ingle recess is reminiscent of those at St. John's (Fig. 224) and Society Hill in Maryland.

In the nineteenth century the medieval style still endured, but in a lessened degree. If you walk on East Bryan Street in Savannah, you will find a tumble-down cottage or quarters with steep roof, winding staircases, vertical board partitions, and open beamed ceilings (Fig. 279). The ancient lines of the dwelling are very evident. Another example of this century is a little old house in Gray (Figs. 276, 280), Jones County, where a transitional "cell" or "aisle" stands at the back of the dwelling. One chimney is covered at its base by a chimney pent, and there is a colonnade and kitchen.

Negro architecture in Georgia is basically in the medieval manner. While a good many of the homes are truly first-class, there are plenty of cottages and shacks, their walls punched with glassless windows, real "wind holes," protected only by board shutters, which are scarcely fit for feudal serfs (Figs. 277, 278). In cities like Macon and Columbus there are lanes upon lanes of tightly packed row huts, reminiscent of English Gothic abodes in the poorer towns.

To Georgia the colonists from England brought no architecture which may be designated pure Gothic. They widely established the English Georgian style of the eighteenth century — to which the great mansions of Savannah bear witness — as well as an old-fashioned style for those days, a survival or hang-over from the Middle Ages, which persisted in Georgia well into the nineteenth century.

But in the Carolinas, in the islands of Bermuda, and particularly in Maryland and Virginia, there flourished during the seventeenth century a pure medieval architecture — occasionally decorated by Jacobean trimmings — which was part and parcel of the English medieval period of the Tower of London, Compton Wynyates, and Westminster Abbey.

How doggedly this style persevered in these colonies into the eighteenth century, and the century which followed, is not generally known. It seems that Americans, especially those of the Old South where traditions are esteemed, have been closer to the heart of medieval England than they realized, as the illustrations of this volume indicate. It has necessitated almost a thousand architectural trips to the back pine woods of the tidewater country over a period of fifteen years to document this medieval strain in the cultural history of this country.

BIBLIOGRAPHY

BIBLIOGRAPHY

Addy, 1933	S. O. Addy. *The Evolution of the English House.* London: Allen and Unwin, 1933.
Ambler, 1913	Louis Ambler. *The Old Halls and Manor Houses of Yorkshire.* London, 1913.
Ambler MSS	Ambler Manuscripts, Library of Congress, Washington.
Am. Phil. Soc. Proc.	*American Philosophical Society Proceedings.*
Andrews, 1934–38	C. M. Andrews. *The Colonial Period of American History.* New Haven: Yale University Press, 1934–38. 4 vols.
Batsford and Fry, 1938	Harry Batsford and Charles Fry. *The English Cottage.* London: Batsford, 1938.
Bemis and Burchard, 1933	A. F. Bemis and J. Burchard. *The Evolving House.* Cambridge, Mass.: Technology Press, 1933–36. Vol. 1.
Blanton, 1930	W. B. Blanton. *Medicine in Virginia in the Seventeenth Century.* Richmond: Byrd Press, 1930.
Braun, 1940	Hugh Braun. *The Story of the English House.* London: Batsford, 1940.
Briggs, 1932	M. S. Briggs. *The Homes of the Pilgrim Fathers in England and America, 1620–1685.* London: Oxford University Press, 1932.
Broadbent, 1931	A. T. Broadbent and A. Minoprio. *The Minor Domestic Architecture of Gloucestershire.* London: Tiranti, 1931.
Brock, 1930	H. I. Brock. *Colonial Churches in Virginia.* Richmond: Dale Press, 1930.
Brown, 1926–37	G. B. Brown. *The Arts in Early England.* London: Murray, 1926–37. 6 vols.
Browning MS	Elizabeth Browning. "Prospero's Palaces, a Study of the Origin and Development of Bermuda's Domestic Architecture." MS submitted to the University of Rochester, New York, in partial fulfillment of the degree of Bachelor of Arts with Distinction, 1939.
Bruce, 1895	P. A. Bruce. *Economic History of Virginia in the Seventeenth Century.* New York, 1895. 2 vols.
Buckinghamshire	*Great Britain. Royal Commission on the Ancient and Historical Monuments and Constructions of England. . . An Inventory of the Historical Monuments in Buckinghamshire.* London, 1912–13. 2 vols.
Bushnell, 1919	D. I. Bushnell, Jr. *Native Villages and Village Sites East of the Mississippi,* Bulletin 69, Bureau of American Ethnology. Washington, 1919.
Calvert Papers	*The Calvert Papers,* no. 1–3. Baltimore, 1889–99.
Clarke, 1923	W. M. Clarke. *Minor English Domestic Architecture.* Los Angeles, 1923.
Coffin and Holden, 1919	L. A. Coffin, Jr., and A. C. Holden. *Brick Architecture of the Colonial Period in Maryland and Virginia.* New York, 1919.

Cooney, 1933   Loraine M. Cooney, comp., and Hattie C. Rainwater, ed., *Garden History of Georgia, 1733–1933*. Atlanta, Ga.: The Peachtree Garden Club, 1933.

Corry, 1930   J. P. Corry. "The Houses of Colonial Georgia," *Georgia Historical Quarterly*, vol. xiv. September, 1930.

Dawber, 1900   E. G. Dawber. *Old Cottages and Farm-houses in Kent and Sussex*. London, 1900.

Dawber, 1905   E. G. Dawber and W. G. Davie. *Old Cottages, Farm-houses, and Other Stone Buildings in the Cotswold District*. London, 1905.

Derb. Arch. Jour.   *Derbyshire Archaeological Journal.*

Ditchfield, 1908   P. H. Ditchfield. *The Charm of the English Village*. London, 1908.

Dutton, 1935   Ralph Dutton. *The English Country House*. London: Batsford, 1935.

EAA   Early American Archives, Library of Congress, Washington.

Earle, 1929   Swepson Earle. *The Chesapeake Bay Country*. Baltimore, 1929. 3rd ed.

Essex   *Great Britain. Royal Commission on the Ancient and Historical Monuments and Constructions of England. . . An Inventory of the Historical Monuments of Essex*. London, 1916–23. 4 vols.

Fletcher, 1924   Banister Fletcher. *A History of Architecture on the Comparative Method*. New York, 1924.

Forman, 1934   H. C. Forman. *Early Manor and Plantation Houses of Maryland*. Easton, Md., and Haverford, Pa.: privately printed, 1934.

Forman, 1938   H. C. Forman. *Jamestown and St. Mary's: Buried Cities of Romance*. Baltimore: Johns Hopkins Press, 1938.

Forman, 1939   H. C. Forman. "Wenlocke Christison's Plantation, The Ending of Controversie," *Maryland Historical Magazine*. September, 1939.

Forman, 1941   H. C. Forman. "The Old Hardware of James Towne," *Antiques Magazine*. January, 1941.

Forman, 1942   H. C. Forman. "The St. Mary's City 'Castle,' Predecessor of the Williamsburg 'Palace,'" *William and Mary Quarterly*, 2nd series, vol. XXII, no. 2. April, 1942.

Garner and Stratton, 1911   Thomas Garner and Arthur Stratton. *The Domestic Architecture of England during the Tudor Period*. London, 1911. 2 vols.

Gotch, 1901   J. A. Gotch. *Early Renaissance Architecture in England*. London, 1901.

Gotch, 1928   J. A. Gotch. *The Growth of the English House*. London, 1928. Revised ed.

Gotch, 1936   J. A. Gotch. *The Old Halls and Manor Houses of Northamptonshire*. London: Batsford, 1936.

Green, 1908   W. Curtis Green, *Old Cottages and Farm-houses in Surrey*. London, 1908.

HABS   Historic American Buildings Survey, Fine Arts Division, Library of Congress, Washington.

Hamor, 1615   Ralph Hamor, *A True Discourse of the Present Estate of Virginia*, London, 1615.

Hening   W. W. Hening, ed. *Statutes at Large . . . a collection of all the laws of Virginia . . .* Richmond, 1810–23. 13 vols.

Herefordshire *Great Britain. Royal Commission on the Ancient and Historical Monuments and Constructions of England. . . An Inventory of the Historical Monuments in Herefordshire.* London, 1931–34. 3 vols.

Holme, 1906 Charles Holme, ed. *Old English Country Cottages.* London, 1906.

Holme, 1915 Charles Holme, ed. *Old English Mansions.* London, 1915.

Humphreys, 1923 J. S. Humphreys. *Bermuda Houses.* Boston, 1923.

Hunter, 1930 R. C. Hunter. *Old Houses in England.* New York: Wiley, 1930.

Huntingdonshire *Great Britain. Royal Commission on the Ancient and Historical Monuments and Constructions of England. . . An Inventory of the Historical Monuments of Huntingdonshire.* London, 1926.

Ingemann, 1938 W. M. Ingemann. *The Minor Architecture of Worcestershire.* London: Tiranti, 1938.

Innocent, 1916 C. F. Innocent. *The Development of English Building Construction.* Cambridge, England, 1916.

Johnson, 1612 Robert Johnson. *The New Life of Virginea.* London, 1612. Reprinted in Peter Force, *Tracts,* I, no. 7, p. 14. Washington, 1835.

Johnston and Waterman, 1941 F. B. Johnston and T. T. Waterman. *The Early Architecture of North Carolina.* Chapel Hill: University of North Carolina Press, 1941.

Jones, 1925 Elias Jones. *History of Dorchester County, Maryland.* Baltimore, 1925. Revised.

Kellam, 1931 S. S. and V. H. Kellam. *Old Houses in Princess Anne, Virginia.* Portsmouth, Va.: Printcraft Press, 1931.

Kelly, 1933 J. F. Kelly. *Early Domestic Architecture of Connecticut.* New Haven: Yale University Press, 1933.

Kimball, 1927 S. F. Kimball. *Domestic Architecture of the American Colonies and of the Early Republic.* New York, 1927.

Kimball, 1935 [S.] F. Kimball, *et al.* "The Restoration of Colonial Williamsburg in Virginia," *Architectural Record,* vol. 78, no. 6. December, 1935.

Kingsbury, 1933 S. M. Kingsbury, ed. *The Records of the Virginia Company of London.* Washington: Govt. Printing Office, 1906–1935. 4 vols.

Leadbeater, 1862 Mary Leadbeater. "The Annals of Ballitore," in *The Leadbeater Papers.* London, 1862.

Lloyd, 1925 Nathaniel Lloyd. *A History of English Brickwork.* London, 1925.

Lloyd, 1931 Nathaniel Lloyd. *A History of the English House from Primitive Times to the Victorian Period.* London: Architectural Press, 1931.

Lockwood, 1931–34 A. G. Lockwood, ed., *Gardens of Colony and State.* New York: Scribner, 1931–34. 2 vols.

Lombard P. H. Lombard. *The Aptucxet Trading Post.* Bourne, Mass., 1934.

London *Great Britain. Royal Commission on the Ancient and Historical Monuments and Constructions of England. . . An Inventory of the Historical Monuments in London.* London, 1924–29. 4 vols.

Lytton E. Bulwer Lytton. *Harold, The Last of the Saxon Kings.* Chicago and New York, n.d.

Mason, April 1939 G. C. Mason. "The Colonial Churches of York County, Virginia," *William and Mary Quarterly,* vol. XIX, no. 2. April, 1939.

Mason, July 1939 G. C. Mason. "The Colonial Churches of Gloucester County, Virginia," *William and Mary Quarterly,* vol. XIX, no. 3. July, 1939.

Mason, 1940   G. C. Mason. "The Colonial Churches of the Eastern Shore of Virginia," *William and Mary Quarterly*, vol. XX, no. 4. October, 1940.

Mason, 1943   G. C. Mason. "The Colonial Churches of Isle of Wight and Southampton Counties, Virginia," *William and Mary Quarterly*, vol. XXIII, no. 1. January, 1943.

Maryland Archives   *Archives of Maryland*. Baltimore: Maryland Historical Society, 1883–.

Messent, 1928   C. J. W. Messent. *The Old Cottages and Farm-houses of Norfolk*. Norwich, England, 1928.

Minutes of Council   *Minutes of the Council and General Court of Colonial Virginia*. Richmond, 1924.

Moorehead, 1934   S. P. Moorehead. "The Castle," *Virginia Magazine of History and Biography*, vol. 42. October, 1934.

Moorehead, 1935   S. P. Moorehead. "Christ's Cross," *Virginia Magazine of History and Biography*, vol. 43. January, 1935.

Morand, 1929   Dexter Morand. *The Minor Architecture of Suffolk*. London, 1929.

Morison, 1935   S. E. Morison. *The Founding of Harvard College*. Cambridge, Mass.: Harvard University Press, 1935.

Moxon, 1703   Joseph Moxon. *Mechanick Exercises*. London, 1703. 3rd ed.

Nevill, 1889   Ralph Nevill. *Old Cottages and Domestic Architecture in South-West Surrey*. Guildford, England, 1889.

Oliver, 1912   Basil Oliver. *Old Houses and Village Buildings in East Anglia, Norfolk, Suffolk, and Essex*. London, 1912.

Oliver, 1929   Basil Oliver. *The Cottages of England, A Review of their Types and Features from the 16th to the 18th Centuries*. London, 1929.

Oswald, 1933   Arthur Oswald. *Country Houses of Kent*. London: Country Life, 1933.

Parker, 1859   J. H. Parker. *Some Account of Domestic Architecture in England, from Richard II to Henry VIII*. Oxford, 1859.

Parkinson, 1904   James Parkinson. *Old Cottages, Farm Houses, and Other Half-Timber Buildings in Shropshire, Herefordshire, and Cheshire*. London, 1904.

Prior, 1900   E. S. Prior. *A History of Gothic Art in England*. London, 1900.

Purchas, 1906   *Purchas His Pilgrimes*. Glasgow, 1906. 20 vols.

Sale, 1927   E. T. Sale. *Interiors of Virginia Houses of Colonial Times*. Richmond, 1927.

Sanford, 1819   Ezekiel Sanford. *The Works of the British Poets*, Philadelphia, 1819.

Shurtleff, 1939   H. R. Shurtleff. *The Log Cabin Myth*. Cambridge, Mass.: Harvard University Press, 1939.

Simpson, 1922   F. M. Simpson. *A History of Architectural Development*. London, 1922. 3 vols.

Sioussat, 1913   A. L. Sioussat. *Old Manors in the Colony of Maryland*, 2nd series. Baltimore, 1913.

Smith, 1884   Capt. John Smith. *Works, 1608–1631*, ed. by Edw. Arber. Birmingham, 1884.

Sparrow, 1909   W. S. Sparrow. *The English House, How to Judge its Periods and Styles*. New York, 1909.

Stanard, 1917   M. N. Stanard. *Colonial Virginia, Its People and Customs.* Philadel-
                             phia, 1917.

Stoney, 1938   S. G. Stoney. *Plantations of the Carolina Low Country.* Charleston:
                             Carolina Art Assn., 1938.

Tilghman, 1915   Oswald Tilghman. *History of Talbot County, Maryland.* Baltimore,
                             1915. 2 vols.

Tipping, 1912   H. A. Tipping, ed. *English Homes of the Early Renaissance; Eliza-
                             bethan and Jacobean Houses and Gardens.* London, 1912.

Tipping, 1924   H. A. Tipping, ed. *English Homes, period II . . . Early Tudor.* Lon-
                             don, 1924.

Trevelyan, 1926   G. M. Trevelyan. *History of England.* London, 1926.

Tyler, 1906   L. G. Tyler. *The Cradle of the Republic: Jamestown and James River*
                             . . . Richmond. 1906.

Upshur and Whitelaw, 1938   A. F. Upshur and R. T. Whitelaw. "Two of the Oldest Brick Dwell-
                             ings in America," *Virginia Magazine of History and Biography,* vol.
                             XLVI. July, 1938.

VMHB   *Virginia Magazine of History and Biography,* Richmond.

Vestry Book, St. Peter's   *Vestry Book and Register of St. Peter's Parish, 1684–1786.* Virginia
                             State Library, Richmond.

Wales and Monmouthshire   *Great Britain. Royal Commission on the Ancient and Historical Monu-
                             ments and Constructions in Wales and Monmouthshire. . . An In-
                             ventory of the Ancient Monuments in Wales and Monmouthshire.*
                             London, 1911–37. 8 vols.

Waterman and Barrows, 1932   T. T. Waterman and J. A. Barrows. *Domestic Colonial Architecture of
                             Tidewater Virginia.* New York: Scribner, 1932.

Waterman, 1946   T. T. Waterman. *The Mansions of Virginia, 1706–1776.* Chapel Hill:
                             University of North Carolina Press, 1946.

Wertenbaker, 1942   T. J. Wertenbaker. *The Old South, The Founding of American Civili-
                             zation.* New York: Scribner, 1942.

Wertenbaker, Golden Age   T. J. Wertenbaker. *The Golden Age of Colonial Culture.* New York:
                             New York University Press, 1942.

Westmorland   *Great Britain. Royal Commission on the Ancient and Historical Monu-
                             ments and Constructions of England. . . An Inventory of the Histori-
                             cal Monuments in Westmorland.* London, 1936.

WMQ   *William and Mary College Quarterly,* Williamsburg, Va.

Wolseley, 1925   Viscountess Wolseley. *Some of the Smaller Manor Houses of Sussex.*
                             London, 1925.

Worthington, 1918   A. F. Worthington. *Twelve Old Houses West of Chesapeake Bay.* Bos-
                             ton, 1918.

Yonge, 1930   S. H. Yonge. *The Site of Old "James Towne,"* Richmond, 1930. 5th
                             ed.

INDEX

Abbot's Hospital, Guildford, England, 146
Abingdon Glebe, 96
Accomac County, 58, 85, 87, 90, 91
Ace of Clubs Church (Pungoteague), 85, 101, 139
Aconbury Church (Herefordshire), 138
Act of 1662, 30
Albemarle Sound, 172
Albion, Earl of, 127
Aldermanbury Street, 119
Alexander Long House (Long's Ferry), 173
All Saints Parish Church (Essex), 128
Allen, Arthur, 58
Allen's Brick House, see Bacon's Castle
American Council of Learned Societies, 108n.
American Revolutionary War, 5, 97, 157
Ampthill, 97
Andros, Sir Edmund, 108
Anglo-Classic style, 4
Anglo-Saxon church, 9, 64, 85; construction, 81;
    palisade, 98, 128, 183; see palisade, wall
Anglo-Saxons, 30, 139
Annapolis, 134n., 145
Anne, Queen, 3, 5
Anne Arundel County, 115, 121, 146, 150, 151,
    156
Aptuxcet Trading Post, 17n.
Ardleigh, 26
Argall, 80
Ashington, 71
Ashley River, 177

Bachelor's Hope, 156
Back Street, 28, 50
Bacon's Castle, 26, 54, 58, 59, 64, 65, 71, 81, 97,
    101, 114, 127, 171, 176, 182; casement
    windows, 65; chimneys, 59; fireplaces, 65;
    pediment, 64
Bacon, Nathaniel, 58, 172
Ballitore, 5
Baltimore, Lord (second), 107, 119; (third), 108,
    113, 144, 151, 156, 158; see Calvert
Baltimore County, 146, 157
Balusters, 127, 138, 162
Banqueting House, Whitehall, 4
Barns, 26, 98, 114
Bathurst, 96

Bathurst, Sir Francis, of Bathurst Bluff, 183
Battle Abbey, house at, 150
Bay (compartment), 15, 36, 99, 100, 121
Belmont, 91
Benedictine monks, 139
Benenden (Kent), 65
Bennett, Richard (Governor), 127
Berkeley, Lady, 30; Sir William (Governor), 26,
    28, 43, 46
Berkeley Plantation, 13, 16, 35, 58
Bethel, 173
Bethesda Orphan House, 183
Bermuda City, 16
Bermuda Islands, 167
Bewdley, 91
Binford House, 91
Birmingham Manor, 115, 156
Bishopstone (Herefordshire), 65
Blackheath (Surrey), 37
Blockhouses, 12, 98
Bloomeries, 98
Bockover House, 173
Bolsover Castle (Derbyshire), 112, 182
Bond Castle, xii, 54, 135, 146, 176; dining room
    of, 138; turned wooden spindles of, 135
Bond, English and Flemish, see brickwork
Boundary Bank Cottage (Westmorland), 20
Bourton-on-the-Water (Gloucestershire), 138
Bower (solar), 5, 25, 26
Bradford Street, Bocking (Essex), 30
Bradford-on-Avon, 64
Bradwell (Essex), 65
Branch, Christopher, 26, 36
Breccles Hall (Norfolkshire), 127
Brewing copper, 37
Brick Billy (Green Oak Farm), 87, 173
Brick Church, Jamestown, 30, 35, 81, 101
Brick enframements, 65
Brick houses, first in Virginia, 17; on James River,
    28; at St. Mary's City, 108; cottages at
    Roanoke Island, 6; see house
Brick nogging, 17, 99, 126
Brick State House of 1676, 134, 135, 171
Bricks, Dutch, 103n., 120; chamfered, 50n.; Eng-
    lish statute, 103n.; watertable (C. quynchon),
    50

Brickwork, black diapered (lozenge), 70, 71, 90, 97, 101, 129, 156, 157, 173; English bonded, 29, 29n., 42n., 97, 147, 151; Flemish bonded, 42; Jacobean, 64; glazed, 42, 50, 70, 90, 150; glazed initials in England and Maryland, 150; kinds of, in Virginia, 102; mousetooth, 47, 59, 102; rubbed (gauged), 42, 50, 70; with chevrons, 50, 90, 129, 151, 173
Bridges Creek, 30
Brill, 64
Brinscome (Surrey), 129
Bristol, 6
Brooke, Robert (Governor), 114
Brooke Place Manor, 151
Broughton, Thomas, 182
Bruce, P. A. (historian), 46
Buckinghamshire, 85
Burwell, Lewis, 59
Butler, Nathaniel (Governor), 167
Buttery (bottlery), 25, 26, 37

Cabin, see house
Calvert, Cecilius, 107, 119; Charles, 108, 151; Leonard, 108, 114; William, 129; see Baltimore, Lord
Calvert County, 114, 118, 126, 127, 129, 135, 147, 151, 154
Calvert House (East St. Mary's), 108
Calvert's Rest, 129
Camden County, 173
Cape Fear River, 172
Capital, at Christ's Cross, 72
Capitol, Williamsburg, 86
Carmarthenshire, 114
Carter's Creek Plantation, see Fairfield
Carter's Grove, 97
Carthagena (expedition), 150; (house), 118, 150
Cascine, 173
Casement, see window
Castle, see Bacon's Castle, Bond Castle, Foster's Castle, Governor's Castle
Caulk's Field, 157
Cecil Friends' Meetinghouse, 114
Cedar Circle, 97
Cedar Hill, 146, 162
Ceiling, tray, 170, 171
Cell (aisle), 90, 147, 157, 173, 184
Chancellor's House at St. Peter's, 108; see Governor's Castle
Chantmarle Manor House (Dorset), 65
Chapel, see church

Chapel of St. Mary's, see St. Mary's Chapel
Charles II, 28
Charles City County, 87
Charles County, 113, 127, 150, 151
Charles' Gift (Preston), 126, 129
Charleston, 177, 182
Chesapeake Bay, 135
Chiddingfold (Surrey), 73
Chimney, "bottled," 170; brick, at Fitzhugh's, 21; crow steps on, 85; flush, 37; T-shaped, 42, 43, 47, 97, 101, 182; of Bacon's Castle, 59; of Governor's Castle, 112; offset, 121; pyramid, 42, 97, 101, 102, 126; stack of brick, 114; wattle, 21, 114; with arches, 97, 135; with diamond stacks, 59, 96, 101, 114; with sunken panels, 91; with square stacks, 72, 73; with withes, 129, 157, 162; wooden (Welsh), 16, 20, 21, 24, 97, 99, 114, 162, 171
Chimney pent (ingle recess), 37, 90, 91, 100, 150, 151, 157, 162, 173, 182, 184
Chowan County, 173
Christian family, 87
Christison (Christopherson), Wenlocke, 128
Christ's Cross (Criss Cross), 54, 71, 72, 101, 146
Church, aisleless nave type, 81, 85, 101; Anglo-Saxon, 85; Argall's, 80; at Ashington (Essex), 71; at Corbridge (Northumberland), 85; at Greenstead (Essex), 98; at St. Margaret Bowers (Essex), 85; at Tollesbury (Essex), 85; at Worth (Sussex), 139; Bermuda, 167; brick, in Virginia, 101; crossroads, 80, 101, 139; cruck, 99; cruciform, 85, 139; English, 138, 167; first, in Virginia, 80; first, on Eastern Shore, 9, 12, 98; first brick, at Jamestown, 80, 81; first Lower, on Eastern Shore, 81; fourth, at Jamestown, 80; in St. Peter's Parish, 87; kinds of, in Virginia, 81; of 1607, 13, 15; of 1610, 15, 80; of 1623, 80; of 1636, 80; oldest wooden, in United States, 144; palisade, 81, 98; parish, 54, 65; Ace of Clubs, 85, 101; Brick, at Jamestown, 30, 35, 81, 101; Old Brick (St. Luke's), 81, 97, 101; Old Trinity, 139; Merchant's Hope, 85; Pungoteague (Ace of Clubs), 85, 101; St. Lawrence, Bishopstone (Herefordshire), 139; Second Bruton Parish, 81, 101
Civil War, 70
Claiborne, 43
Clapboards, 17
Clay, Henry, 128
Clay's Neck, 126, 128

Clegg Hall (Lancashire), 112
Clemson, 182
Clocker, Daniel, 126
Clocker's Fancy, 118, 126, 128
Clover Fields, 154
Cluster Cottage, 170
Coat of arms, 43
Cocke, Thomas, 70
Colemere (Shropshire), 15
College, at Henrico, 98
Compton Wynyates (Warwickshire), 72, 134, 184
Cooper, Sir Anthony, 177
Cooper River, 177
Constitution, United States, 151
Construction, Indian, 99; medieval types of, in
    Virginia, 98; post-and-beam, 91, 103, 114,
    144, 157; wattle, 81, 98, 99; see house, wall
Copley, Sir Lionel, 108
Corbridge church (Northumberland), 85
Cornish houses, 21, 100
Cornwaleys, Thomas, 107, 108
Corotoman, 90
Cottage, see house
Cottage Farm, 157
Council Chamber, 119
Country-Ludwell-State House block, Jamestown, 30
Court House, Talbot County (1680), 96n., 115,
    134, 135; (1709), 141; (1711), 146
Court House Room, 70
Court of guard, 98, 108
Courtyard, 112
Cradle House (Essex), 71, 118
Crakehon, 13
Cross Manor (Manor of Cornwaleys Crosse), 156
Cross-house, 54, 65, 70, 71, 72, 87, 101, 134;
    see house
Cruck, 9, 13, 15, 37, 99, 115
Cupola, 112
Cupola House, 176
Curtain, 64, 101, 102, 127, 150
Custis House, 87, 103

Dahl's Swamp (Topping House), 90, 104
Dairies, 114
Daren Farm (Herefordshire), 13
D'Arsens, Jean, 177
Darwin (Lancashire), 21
Davis house, 173
DeCourcy, Henry, 129
Delaware, Lord, 15, 80
Delft tiles, 35

Dependencies, see outbuildings
Derbyshire, 25, 112, 182
Devonshire (Bermuda), 171
Diamond stacks, see chimney
Door, of match boards, 146; Tudor, in Virginia,
    72, 101
Doorway, battlemented, 71, 72, 101; claddings
    for, 4
Dorchester County, 156
Dorset, 65
Dovecot, 26, 96
Dr. Lucas House, 91, 104
Drummond, William (Governor), 172
Duke of Gloucester Street, 96
Dumfries, 97

Earlham Hall, 178
East Anglian cottage, 100
East Bryan Street, Savannah, 184
East India College, 98
East St. Mary's, see Calvert House
Eastern Shore (Maryland), 114, 115, 126, 127,
    128; (Virginia), 9, 12, 81, 98, 139
Easton, 144
Eastwood, 103
Edenton, 176
Edward IV, 112
Elizabeth, Queen, 3, 5, 13
Elizabeth City, 173
Ending of Controversie, The, 126, 128
English bond, see brickwork
Essex, 17, 30, 35, 50, 51, 58, 64, 71, 72, 85, 96,
    115, 118, 126, 128, 134

Fairfax, Lord, 151
Fairfield, 59, 71, 96, 97
Fassit House, 146, 157
Fauntleroy, William, 58
Federal Grove, 154
Field of the Cloth of Gold, 3, 4, 5
Fire-house, Norse, 25
Fireplace, back-to-back, 30, 119, 182; cater-cor-
    nered, 147, 150, 156, 157; hooded, 65; kinds
    of, in Virginia, 103; kitchen, 70; largest, in
    Maryland, 120; side, 35; with seats, 37; see
    chimney
First State House, Jamestown, 28, 29, 30, 35, 100,
    119
Fisher House, 90
Fishing Point, 81
Fitzhugh, William, 21

Flemish bond, *see* brickwork

Floors, earth, 5, 16; kinds of, in Virginia, 103

Fort, in Bermuda, 167; Eustis, 72; of Federico, 183; James, 9, 12, 15, 98; St. George's, 6; St. Mary's, 115, 119

Foster, Colonel Joseph, 71

Foster's Castle, 54, 71, 72, 101, 146, 176

Fourth State House, Jamestown, 54, 65, 70, 101

Fox's Harbor, 160

France, brickwork patterns from, 71

Francis I, 3

Frank Leslie's Illustrated Weekly, 64

Frederico, fort of, 183

Freeland, Thelbert, house of, 151

Friends, Society of, 144

Frosbury (Surrey), house near, 134

Gables, design of, 90, 102; row, 29, 30, 119; Flemish or Jacobean, 58, 101, 102, 170, 171, 177, 182; steepest in Virginia, 90

Gaines Farm Quarters, 91

Gainsborough Old Hall (Lincolnshire), 37

Galehouse Farm (Essex), 126

Gambrel, *see* roof

Gantt family, 146

Gantt House, *see* Cedar Hill

Gardens, 97, 98, 134

Gaston County, 176

Gates County, 172, 176

Gatley Park (Herefordshire), 112

General Assembly, 28

Genezir, 151, 157

George Washington Birthplace National Monument, 30

Georgia, early settlement of, 183

Georgian mansion, 36, 90, 96, 97, 100, 104, 145, 157, 173, 184; *see* house

Georgian period, 4, 50, 145

Georgian stairway, 127

Ghent, Skipper's House, 58

Gillow Manor (Herefordshire), 127

Glass, 4, 87, 119, 146, 170; *see* quarrel

Glassworks, 98

Glazed brick, *see* brickwork

Glebe House, Littlepage's, 87. *See also*, Abingdon Glebe

Gloucester County, 59, 96, 97

Gloucestershire, 37, 96, 138

Gothic Revival, 97, 103, 157

Governor, of Bermuda, 167; of Maryland, 114, 129; of Virginia, 43, 127

Governor's Castle (St. Peter's), 108, 112, 147, 158

Governor's Council, 171

Governor's Garden, Jamestown, 36

Governor's House, Jamestown, 43

Governor's Palace, 86, 112, 158

Graeme House, 147, 152

Gray (Georgia), 184

Gray, Reverend Arthur, 71n.

Gray family, 127

Grange Farm, 94

Grass wall, *see* wall

Great Hall, 43, 65, 100, 147, 173. *See also*, hall

Great House, 5, 25

Great Yarmouth, 43

Green County, 184

Green Oak Farm, *see* Brick Billy

Green Park, 151

Green Spring, the, 26, 46, 64; description of, 43

Greenstead-by-Ongar (Essex), 12, 98

Greenway, 87, 88

Greenwood, 154

Gregory House, 173

Groombridge Place (Kent), 86

Grove Hill, 97

Guest house, 16, 98

Guildford, 146

"Guillotine," *see* window

Gunn's Run, 87

Haddon Hall, 128

Half-and-half work, *see* house

Half-timberwork, 6

Hall (great room), 26, 37, 58, 100, 101, 115, 127, 147, 173; meaning of, 25; the medieval, 4; Yorkshire, 4

Hall, James, house of, 121

Hall, Joseph (Bishop), 36, 121

Hall-and-parlor house, *see* house

Hamilton Parish (Bermuda), houses in, 171

Hampton, Reverend Thomas, 80

Hampton Court Palace, 71, 91

Hampton houses, Jamestown, 35

Hanover, 182

Hanover County, 91

Hardware, 29, 35, 37

Harmony Hall, 145

Harold, the Saxon, 21

Harrington Sound, house at, 171

Harvard College, 108
Harvey, Sir John, 28
Hastings, Battle of, 12
Hatton's Mansion (Chapel Hill), 160
Hearth, central, 4, 21, 25
Hebb, William, 150
Hebden's Point, 114
Hellens Dovecote (Herefordshire), 150
Hemington (Leicestershire), 15
Henrico (Henricopolis), 9, 16, 17, 98
Henrico County, 54, 58, 70
Henry VIII, 3, 5, 21
Herefordshire, 13, 25, 30, 35, 85, 127, 138, 139, 150
High Birk House (Westmorland), 20
Hobbeville, 173
Holly Hill, 115, 121, 146
Holmwood, John, 58
Holmwood's dwelling, 35
Holy Trinity, Bradwell (Essex), 138
Hope Farm (Herefordshire), 138
House, "advanced" central-passage type, 47, 50; at Turkey Island, 54; brick, at Jamestown, 30; brick, in Virginia, 99; central-passage type, 47, 50, 129, 146, 157, 172, 173; Cotswold, 126; cross-, 54, 58, 70, 71, 87, 101, 134, 146, 159, 167, 170, 171; country, in Virginia, 36, 54, 100; country, in Maryland, 121, 158, 159, 162; cruck, 13, 15, 99; double-parlor, 43, 44; English, 13, 15, 25, 113; "fair English," 99; first brick, in Virginia, 17; first brick, in Maryland, 158; first type of, in Maryland, 121; flax, 35; flimsy, at St. Mary's City, 107; half-and-half, 17, 99, 115, 127; half-and-parlor, 37, 38, 43, 59, 87, 100, 126, 127, 128, 146, 172, 173; gambrel roofed, in North Carolina, 173; Georgian, 96, 97, 145 (see Georgian mansion); Great, 25, 26; guest, 16; in Jamestown, 1611, 99; Jacobean, in England, 158; Jacobean, in Bermuda, 171; Jacobean, in North Carolina, 176; log, 6; London, 100; manor, in England, 26; manor, in Maryland, 113; Maryland medieval, characteristics of, 158, 159, 162; Norse, 25; of Christopher Branch, 36; of William May, 43; of William Sherwood, 43; of Thomas Cornwaleys, 107; of Richard Wright, 115; one-bay, 37, 100; 121; ox, 15; puncheoned, 98, 167, 183; row, 28, 30, 35, 119, 158, 159, 167; salt-box,
147; stock sizes of, in Jamestown, 96; stock size of, in Virginia, 28; thatched, 115; timber-framed, 99, 107, 108, 115, 119, 135, 167, 172, 176; town, 28, 36, 100, 119, 158, 176; transitional, 90, 96, 103, 104, 145, 147, 150, 151, 156, 162, 173, 182; two-storied, 91; two kinds of, in Savannah, 183; typical London, 28; typical, in Virginia, 43; with cell, 90
House, Adam Thoroughgood, 100
"House on Isaac Watson's Land," 36, 37, 100
"House on the Lands of Mr. John Watson and Mr. Knight," 50
House, Piney Neck, 114
House of Records, Maryland, 119
Huggins House, 90
Huntingdonshire, 58
Hurst Green (Sussex), house at, 118

Ingle recess, see chimney pent

Jacobean baluster, 138; door head, 138; enframements, 65; gables, 58, 101, 170; pediment, 64, 101; porch, 46, 146; stair, 127
Jail, Talbot County, 115
James I, 58
James City, see Jamestown
James City County, 43, 47, 90, 97
James Fort, 9, 12, 15, 98
James River, 12, 13, 16, 17, 42, 58, 70, 80, 98, 156
Jamestown (James City), 6, 9, 15, 16, 17, 20, 28, 30, 35, 36, 37, 43, 50, 54, 65, 70, 80, 81, 96, 99, 100, 101, 107, 119, 167, 172, 183
Jamestown Brick Church, 81; see Brick Church
Jamestown Island, 9; list of buildings between 1607 and 1620, 98
Jenifer, Daniel of St. Thomas, 151
Jetty (overhang), 135, 156, 162, 176
John Roberts House, 172
John's Point, 156
Jones, Francis, 171
Jones, Inigo, 4, 96
Jones County, 184
Jones House, see Matthew Jones House
Jutland (St. Elizabeth's Manor), 129

Keeling House, 47, 50, 90, 101, 129
Kennebec River, 6
Kentshire, 65, 86, 126, 128
Kent County, 115, 156, 157
King Carter's plantation, 90

King William County, 91, 96, 97
King's Council, 9
Kis Kis Kiack, 47, 101
Kitchen, 183; buildings in the South, 26
Knight, Mr., house of, 50
Knott, James, 25

Ladder, 147, 172
Lamb's Meadows, 156
Lancashire, 21
Lancaster County, 90, 91
Lankford House, 146
Larkin, John, 151
Larkin's Hills (Lark's Hills), 151
Latches, 5
Latchley's Manor House (Essex), 50, 65
Latrobe, Benjamin H., 46, 64
Lean-to, 147; see cell, outshut
Leicestershire, 15
Leigh House, 121
Library of Congress, 70
Lincolnshire, 37
Linsey, James, 113
Little Hereford (Herefordshire), 127
Little Riddick House, 172
Little Warley Hall (Essex), 7, 134
Little Wenham Hall (Suffolk), 35, 65
Littlefield Farms (Surrey), 134
Littlepage, 87; house of, 21
Littleton, Southey, 58
Lloyd family, 129
Lloyd's Landing Farm, 146
Lock Leven, 160
Locke, John, 177
Lockey, Edward, house of, 58
Log house (log cabin), 6, 9, 108; see house
London, 4, 16, 20, 28, 29, 30, 36, 46, 86, 167;
    typical house in, 28; house plans of, 100
Long Lane Farm, 126, 127
Long's Ferry, 173
Longtown (Herefordshire), 13
"Lost Lady" (play by Berkeley), 46
Louisburg, 173
Louvers, 21
Lower Brockhampton (Herefordshire), 127
Lower Church, first on Eastern Shore, 81; see
    church
Lower Marston (Herefordshire), 65, 138
Lucas, see Dr. Lucas House
Ludwell, Thomas, 26
Lynch, house near, 160

Maine, 6
Makepeace, 129
Malvern Hill (battle), 70; (house), 54, 70, 71,
    72, 101, 134, 151; see also Mulberry Hill
Manor, 26, 113; houses, 114; in South Carolina,
    177
Manor Farm (Herefordshire), 127; (Essex), 51
Manor of Cornwaleys' Crosse, see Cross Manor
Mansion Hall, 126, 127
Marksall (Essex), 71
Maryland, capitol (1654), 126; manor, 113;
    oldest brick house, 156; religious freedom,
    107, 128; southern, 126; Tercentenary, 134;
    town house, 119; types of medieval wall con-
    struction, 115. See Part III, Chapters I–VIII
Mason and Dixon Line, 3
Massachusetts, 17, 107, 128
Mattapany Street, 139
Matthew Jones House, 54, 72, 73, 87, 114
May, William, 36, 100
Mechanick Exercises, by Moxon, 28
Medieval style, see style
Medway, 177
Meetinghouse, Cecil Friends', 114
Meetinghouses, crossroads, in Maryland, 144
Meetinghouse, Old Gunpowder Friends', 157
Merchant House, 97
Merchant's Hope Church, 85
Merriwether, Major Nicholas, 87
Middle Plantation, 81
Middlebury, 182
Middleton Place, 182
Midhurst (Sussex), 30
Midway Church, 183
Mill, St. Mary's City, 108
Mill's Point, 146
Mistake, The, 154
Moat, 6, 12
Moldings, Gothic, 72, 127, 138
Montague House, 87
More, Richard (Governor), 167
Morison, Samuel E., 13
Moxon, 28
Mt. Eagle, 150
Mt. Pleasant, 160
Mulberry Castle, 182
Mulberry Grove, 126
Mulberry Hill (Malvern Hill), 151
Mulliken's Delight, 146
My Lord's Gift, 129

Neale, James, 113
Negro houses in Georgia, 184
Nether Hall (Essex), 71
New England, 6
New Hall (England), 43
New Kent County, 21, 24, 54, 71, 86, 87, 91, 99
New York, 91
Newfoundland, 6
Nicholson, Sir Francis, 108, 112
Norfolk (England), 30, 86, 127
Norfolk (Virginia), 42, 100
Norman Conquest, 29
Normandy, 42
North Carolina, 6; early settlements in, 172
North Chachan, stable at, 182
Northampton (house), 151
Northampton County, 90
Northamptonshire, 65
Northborough Manor (Northamptonshire), 65
Northumberland, 85

Oak Grove, 176
Obligation Farm, 150
Old Bloomfield, 146
Old Brick Church (St. Luke's), 81, 85, 97, 101, 139, 176
Old Brick House, 173
Old Charles Town (Old Town), 177
Old Mulberry (Mulberry Castle), 182
Old Point Comfort, 9
Old Town, houses at, 177
Old Trinity Church, 139
Old Williams Home, 171
Oldcourt Farm (Herefordshire), 13, 15, 25, 26, 30, 35
Ongar (Essex), 12
Outbuildings (outhouses), 26, 97, 114, 170
Outshut, 37, 102; see cell, lean-to
Oven, Dutch, 37
Oxford (England), 28; (Talbot County), 146

Palace of St. John's, 109
Paget, 170, 171
Paget, Lord, 171
Painting, mural, 138
Palisade, 6, 9, 12, 15, 27, 98, 115, 128; at Jamestown, 80; at St. Mary's Fort, 108; in Georgia, 183; in Virginia churches, 81; see wall
Palladio, 4
Pallant House, 130
Paneling, Gothic linen-fold, 59

Pantile, see roof, tile
Pargetry, 17, 43, 103
"Park-pales," 12
Parker, John, 25
Parliament, Act of, 29
Parrott, William, 127
Parrott's Cage, 126, 127
Parsonage Farm (Herefordshire), 138
Part-brick-and-part-framing, 9; see house (half-and-half)
Pasquahanza, 129
Paul Jones House, 151
Pediment (incipient or embryonic), 64, 81, 97, 101, 102, 171
Pemberton Hall, 151
Pembrokeshire, 21
Pendell (Surrey), 96
Penn, William, 144
Pepys, Samuel, 46
Perquimans County, 173
Petworth (Sussex), 129
Philadelphia, 177
Pilgrim Fathers, 6, 9, 98
Pinnacle Row (Norfolk), 30
Piney Neck House, 114
Pinewoods (Warburton House), 47, 59, 90, 101, 173
Pirate House, 157
Pitchford Hall (Shropshire), 138
Pitt County, 173
Pitt's Bridge, 146
Plan (floor), cross, in England, 139; formal, 156; in England and Virginia, 29; Jacobean, in South Carolina, 182; of churches in Virginia, 81; of Jamestown houses, 35; of Medway, 177; of the Governor's Castle, 108; square, in Maryland and England, 112; seventeenth-century type of, 91; stock, at Jamestown, 100; T-shaped, 71, 96, 156; of a "town house," St. Mary's, 119
Plantation, see manor
Plaster, 17, 43, 103
Plymouth (Massachusetts), 9, 98, 107, 128
Pocahontas, 50
Poindexter, George, 71
Point Pleasant, 92
Porch (enclosed), 58, 64, 70, 71, 101, 115, 134, 146, 156, 170, 171; at the Green Spring, 46; origin of, in Anglo-Saxon church, 64; with turned spindles, in England and Maryland, 135, 138

Porch, entrance, 54
Porch, inset, 156
Porch, Jacobean, 46
Porch chamber, 58, 70
Potomac River, 30
Potter, Henry, house of, 113
Preston, 126, 129; see Charles' Gift
Prince George County, 85
Prince George's County, 145, 146, 151, 156, 157
Princess Anne County, 42, 47, 90, 100
Protestant, 107
Puncheons (punches), 9, 12, 13, 27, 98, 115, 183; see wall
Pungoteague (Ace of Clubs) Church, 85, 101, 139
Pyramid, see chimney, roof

Quarrel (leaded glass), 29; first, discovered in Maryland, 119; first, discovered in Virginia, 46; see glass
Quarters (puncheons), 12; (slave), 114
Queen Anne's County, 129, 145

Raleigh (North Carolina), 173
Raleigh, City of, on Roanoke Island, 6
Raleigh, Sir Walter, 6
Randolph family, 54
Rappahannock River, 58
Raynham Park (Norfolk), 86
Rebellion, Bacon's, 58
Religious freedom in Maryland, 158; see Maryland
Renaissance, 3, 4
Resurrection Manor, 121, 126, 127
Retreat, The, 151
Reveal West House, 91
Revolution, American, 5, 97, 157
Rich Neck Manor, 142
Richardson House, 90, 92
Riddle's Bay, house near, 171
Ringfield, 91, 104
Ripley Manor House (Surrey), 64, 171
Road View Kitchen, 21, 97
Roanoke Island, 6, 172
Rock Hall, 16
Rodd Court (Herefordshire), 134
Rolfe, John, 50; Thomas, 50
Roman Catholics in Maryland, 107, 139
Roman villas, 12
Roof, bark, 99; Bermuda, 170; catslide, 90, 91, 147; covered with boards, 13; Dutch, 91; gambrel, 91, 151, 173, 182; hip ("pyra-
mid"), 96, 134, 147, 156, 171; "Italian," early example of, in Maryland, 135; Jacobean, 182; jerkin, 96, 156; kinds of, in Virginia, 103; mansard, 85; of Snow Hill Manor, 115; palmetto, 167; pantile, 29, 108, 134; shingle, 183; shingle-tile, 29, 112; steepest in Virginia, 90; thatched, 13, 15, 27, 29, 99, 115; with cupola, 112; with pitch of 55 degrees, 47
Roofed ingle, see chimney pent
Rose Croft, 151
Rose Garden, 92
Rosedale, 157
Rowan County, 173, 176
Roydon (Essex), 71

Saffron Walden (Essex), 17
St. Andrew (Essex), 12, 71
St. Aylott's (Essex), 17
St. Barbara's (Troughton-Brome house), 151
St. Clair's Hall (Essex), 30
St. Edmund, 12
St. Elizabeth's Manor (Jutland), 129
St. George, houses in, 171
St. George's, Bermuda, 167
St. George's (Pungoteague Church), 85; see Ace of Clubs Church
St. George's Fort, 6
St. John's (house), 150, 184
St. John's, Palace of, 108
St. Lawrence (Herefordshire), Church of, 139
St. Lawrence, Church of, at Bradford-on-Avon, 64
St. Luke's (Old Brick Church), 91, 101
St. Margaret Bowers church (Essex), 85
St. Mary's Chapel, 108, 139
St. Mary's City, 107, 108, 112, 115, 118, 121, 126, 134, 139, 147, 150, 151, 157, 158, 159, 171; early brick residences in, 108; wooden chimneys in, 114; instructions for laying out, 119
St. Mary's County, 114, 121, 127, 129, 146, 150, 151, 156, 157
St. Mary's Fort, 115, 119
St. Mary's River, 118, 134
St. Mary's Road, 139
St. Peter's, see Governor's Castle
St. Peter's Church, 21
St. Peter's Key, 121n.
St. Peter's Parish, 86, 87
St. Richard's Manor, 150
St. Stephen's Parish Church, 182

St. Thomas Jenifer, Daniel of, 151
Saling Hall (Essex), 58
Salisbury, 173
Salisbury Plain, 91
Sandgates, 150
Sandys Parish, house in, 171
Santee-Cooper Reservoir, 182
Savannah, 183, 184
Scalegate (Westmorland), 20
Scotland, outshuts in, 37
Second Bruton Church, 81, 101
Secretary, of Virginia, 70
Secretary's Office (Council Chamber), 119
Seigneur de Weirnhoudt, 177
Seven Springs, 96
Shakespeare, 167
Sheriff of Henrico County, 70
Sherwood mansion, 43
Shropshire, 43
Shutters, 29, 146
Simpson, Paul, house of, 113, 114
Skiff's Creek House, 90, 103
Skipper's House, Ghent, 58
Smith, Captain John, 13, 167
Smith's Fort Plantation, 50
Smith's Town House, 116
Snow Hill Manor, 114, 115, 157
Snowden, Richard, Jr., 156
Snowden family, 115
Society Hill, 184
Solar (bower), 25
Somers, Sir George, 167
Somerset County, 129, 145, 146, 157
South Carolina, first settlement in, 177
Southampton County, 91
Springfield, 124, 157
Stacks, see chimney
Stair tower, 54, 65, 70
Staircase, winding (boxed or sealed), 37, 43, 70, 87, 91, 115, 128, 144, 147, 150, 151, 156, 157, 162, 173, 184; in Virginia, 102; in Maryland and England, 126; development in England, 127; Jacobean, 127; open well, 65, 135; with handrail, 156
Star Chamber, Great Yarmouth, 43
State House, Bermuda, 167; timber-framed, at St. Mary's City, 112; see Brick State House of 1676, First State House, Third State House, Fourth State House
Steeple Bumpstead (Essex), 50

Stigerwalt House, 176
Storehouse, in Bermuda, 167; in St. Mary's City, 108
Stratford Hall, 97
Street, Duke of Gloucester, 96; see Aldermanbury Street, Back Street, Mattapany Street
Stibbington Hall (Huntingdonshire), 58
Strachey, William, 17, 20, 21, 25
Style, Georgian, in Georgia, 184; in Maryland, 147, 162; in Virginia, 86, 90
Style, Gothic Revival, 97, 103, 157
Style, medieval, summary of, in Virginia, 98ff.; summary of, in Maryland, 158ff.; in Bermuda, 167; in Georgia, 183, 184; in North Carolina, 172; in South Carolina, 177
Style, transitional, in Maryland, 162; in Virginia, 86
Suffolk, 35
Sulgrave Manor, 73
Summerfield, 146
Sussex, 37, 118
Surrey (England), 13, 37, 43, 73
Surry County (Virginia), 50, 54
Sweet Air, 157
Sweet Hall, 43

Tabb House, 86, 87, 90, 103
Talbot County, 115, 128, 134, 144, 146, 147; see Court House, jail
Tankfield, cross-house, 170; stone cottage at, 170
Tatershall Castle, 120
Tempest, The, 167
"Thatcht" house, 115; see house
Thelbert Freeland's House, 151
Third Haven Meetinghouse, 144, 145
Third State House, Jamestown, 30, 54, 65
Thomas Thornton dwelling, 90
Thomas White house, 173
Thornton, Thomas, 90
Thornton house, 184
Thoroughgood House, Adam, 42, 47, 50, 54, 90, 100
Three Sisters, 151
Tile, 17, 29, 35, 103, 112, 134; see roof
Timber-framing, 6, 9, 16, 27, 99, 115; see house, wall
Tobacco house, 114
Tobacco Stick Creek, 156
Toddsbury, 91
Tollesbury (Essex), church at, 85

Topping House, *see* Dahl's Swamp
Tower of London, 65, 184
Towles, Henry, Junior, 90
Towles Point, 90, 104
"Town house within the Fort," St. Mary's City, 119
"Town House," Bermuda, 167
Tray ceiling, 170, 171
Treasury, Annapolis, 134n.; Lord Baltimore's, 113
Troughton-Brome house, *see* St. Barbara's
Tudor period, 91
Turkey Island dwelling, 54
Turkey Neck, 151
Tyler, John, 87
Ty-Mawr (Herefordshire), 13

Upper Bennett, 118, 127

Vaillant House, 146
Virginia, 6, 172, 173, 176, and Part II, Chapters I–X; five types of English medieval architecture in, 9; North (Maine), 6
Virginia Company, 6, 16, 28

Wainscot, in Maryland and England, 128
Wake County, 173
Wakefield, 173
Wall, battlemented brick, in Virginia, 28; brick nogged, 17; grass (sedge), 13, 17, 99; "half-and-half," 17; Indian, 99; kinds of, in Virginia, 103; in Maryland, 115; crenelated, 6; of shingle tiles, 17; palisaded, 12, 27, 115, 128; party, 29; plaster, 17; puncheoned, 13, 27, 98, 115; thicknesses of, 29; timber-framed, 16, 27; wattle, 17; weatherboard, 17
Walnut Grove, 145, 147
Walton House (Chowan County), 173; (Gates County), 173
Want Water, 156
Warburton House, *see* Pinewoods
Wardes Otham (Kent), 126
Warwick (Bermuda), 170, 171
Warwick County, 54, 72
Warwickshire, 134
Washington, George, 30; John, 30; Lawrence, 150; of Sulgrave Manor, 73
Watchtowers, 12
Water table, 50; *see* brickwork
Watervale (Windsor Shade), 91

Watson, Isaac, 36, 37; John, 50
Wattles, 6, 12, 13, 17, 20, 21, 27, 81, 98, 99, 114; *see* walls, chimney
Welsh chimney, *see* chimney
West End Farm (Surrey), 73
West St. Mary's, 150
Westminster Abbey, 184
Westmorland, 20, 50, 128
Westward (Lancashire), 37
Westover, 97
Wharton Court (Herefordshire), 150
White, Thomas, house of, 173
White Birch, 157
White Hall, 147
Whitehall (Huntingdonshire), 58; (London), 4, 86
White-Newbold House, 173
Wicket, 162
Wicomico County, 151
Wilkinson, Dr. Henry, 171n.
William May's House, 100
William the Conqueror, 65
Williams Point, 154
Williamsburg, 70, 81, 87, 96, 101, 112, 158
Wiltshire, Sheriff of, 64
Winchester, 64
Window, arched, 97, 101, 151, 173
Window, casement, 5, 37, 42, 46, 59, 65, 71, 80, 101, 102, 119, 134, 135, 145, 146, 147, 177; at Governor's Castle, 108; at Holly Hill, 115; in Maryland, 115; in Virginia, 29, 30; in Yorkshire, 87
Window, cellar, 65
Window, "guillotine," 86, 145, 146
Window, lie-on-your-stomach, 42, 43, 101, 102, 126, 127, 128, 129, 146, 151
Window, *oeil-de-boeuf* (bull's-eye), 71, 81, 101, 176
Window, pointed-arched, 101, 139
Window, sash, 50, 86, 87, 103, 144, 146, 147, 156, 162
Windsor, 24
Windsor Forest, 154
Windsor Shade, *see* Watervale
Wingfield, Edward Maria, 9
Winona, 59
Wishart House, 42, 91, 100
Wolleston Manor, 113
Wolsey, Cardinal, 71
Wood House Farm (Herefordshire), 13

Wooden chimney, *see* chimney
Woodham Walter Church (Essex), 85
Worcester County, 146, 151, 157
Worth (Essex), church at, 139
Wright, Richard, house of, 115
Wright family, 150
Wroxham (Norfolkshire), 64
Wye House, 126, 129

Wye River, 115
Wythe House, 173

Yeocomico Church, 82
York, wooden chimneys at, 21
York County, 47, 86
York River, 42
Yorkshire, 4, 59, 87